fresh!

market people and their food

Photography by Caro Llewellyn

ARO LLEWELLYN

Random House Australia Pty Ltd
20 Alfred Street, Milsons Point, NSW 2061

Sydney, New York, Toronto,
London, Auckland, Johannesburg
and agencies throughout the world

First published in 1996

National Library of Australia
Cataloguing-in-Publication Data

Llewellyn, Caro, 1965-.
  Fresh! market people and their food.

  ISBN 0 09 183264 0.

  1. Cookery. 2. Markets Australia. I. Title

  641.5

Illustrations by Luisa Laino
Text design by Mary Callahan and Luisa Laino
Typeset by Luisa Laino
Printed in Hong Kong by Dah Hua Printing

Contents

Acknowledgments

There have been many people without whose help this book would not have been possible.

Firstly I would like to thank all the people who have shared their culinary secrets with me. I was invited to people's homes, I was able to taste and try, I was given recipes that I believe to be great secrets. The Italian and Greek communities welcomed me warmly into their culinary worlds and I hope this book helps to keep alive their spirit, generosity and warmth. I would also like to thank:

• My agent Fiona Inglis at Curtis Brown who continues to support and encourage my ideas, who is never failing in her willingness to help and offer guidance.

• Margaret Sullivan, my publisher, who was committed to the idea of a cookbook that looked beyond recipes to cultures whose influence on Australia has been important.

• Brigid Costello who lent me her camera and taught me about depth of field the day before I left to start this project.

• Marisa Wilkins who I can say without doubt is the best cook I know. Marisa carefully went through each recipe with me. She taught me a great deal about Italian food and for that, her friendship, and all the assistance she gave to this project, I give thanks.

• Amanda, Jane and Emma who had me to stay in their beautiful home.

• Great thanks to Richard and Becky Llewellyn who first took me to the Port Adelaide market and introduced me to many of the people in this book. Thanks too for planting the seed of this idea in my mind and for all your help in collecting recipes.

• Amanda O'Connell, whose sensitive and intelligent editing has made this a better book.

• Mary Callahan and Luisa Laino's work on the design and layout of this book has been inspiring, making the words and pictures wonderful to look at.

Many thanks to Jennifer Steele who made the publicity shoot a lot of fun and for her patience in making me feel at ease and for her skill behind the camera and then in the darkroom, I'm grateful.

To dear Jack, whose cheerfulness and co-operation on these expeditions was astounding. I hope you remember these trips with fondness and know that none of this would have been possible without you having made it the joy it was.

Introduction

Fresh! is a book born not from expertise but from a number of my personal loves. Seeds for careers and ways of life or ideas are often planted long before they become manifest. So if you ask, why this book? what gave me the idea? the answer lies in a series of events that started back as long ago as my primary school days.

My best friend at Rose Park Primary School was Mary. Her parents were first-generation migrants from Italy and I remember the first time I went back to her house after school. I rushed home and exclaimed to my mother, 'Mary's got groceries growing in the backyard!'

My mum laughed and explained the definition of groceries which I didn't much care about — all I knew was that Mary's vegetable garden was like nothing I'd ever seen before. The backyards I was used to only ever had a bit of grass and a few trees so Mary's place was something really special.

We used to rollerskate down the concrete path alongside rows of tall tomato plants and along the verandah under heavy canopies of dark grapes. Mary's mother would sit on a chair shelling peas for the evening meal and tell us not to eat too many grapes as we skirted past her with big bunches in our hands, our cheeks bulging. When she wasn't looking we'd steal handfuls of the sweet peas she'd just shelled then lie through green teeth about what we'd done.

At school I was always trying to swap sandwiches with Mary and still remember the fantastic thick slices of bread filled with cured meats and pickled vegetables her mum wrapped up for her each morning.

Another interlude that led me to this project took place when I was at high school — I got a job working at the Adelaide markets at what was then the only organic fruit and vegetable stall at the markets. I loved my job there because the place was so alive — and ever since I have loved going to produce markets.

The atmosphere at a market is exciting and forces you to abandon shopping lists, to go with the flow, talk, try and experience. You may leave home wanting to marinate mushrooms but be drawn to the stall over there in the corner where the woman is yelling, 'Asparagus, come on! Three bunches, two dollars.' You walk over expecting (for that price) the quality to be poor, but find instead crisp, tender young stalks beckoning you to forget about the mushrooms. What's best of all is that if you don't know how to marinate them, chances are the person selling them is an expert and only too happy to share her knowledge.

This was how I collected the recipes for this book. I walked up and down the rows of trestle tables or stalls at lots of markets and asked people how they cooked at home. So many people I spoke to said at first, 'We not do anything special. We just use what we got, you know, what's in the garden…what's in the fridge.'

Fortunately, the climatic similarities between Australia, Greece and Italy have enabled the people who share their recipes in this book to cook largely in the same way they did in the countries of their birth — using an abundance of fresh vegetables, seafood and meats. Once people started talking it was clear that though 'nothing special' might mean 'nothing fancy', their recipes were a wonderful showcase of simplicity, flavour and tradition.

It is my feeling, though, that many of these old traditions will soon be lost as second and third generations' cooking styles and tastes are influenced by Australian culture.

It's not only that the traditions will be lost within these families that is sad; there's also the loss to Australia where the current fad is for highly structured cooking that often looks more like a plastic facsimile of the original ingredients — it is so perfect — rather than something to eat. Sometimes I feel this style of cooking, while looking good, is far removed from the ideas of warmth and generosity that food is meant to represent. To me, much of what we are served in our best restaurants looks classy, but it also looks cold and austere — soulless.

At the other end of the spectrum, are the pre-packaging, cold stores and fast foods that are alienating us from real produce. It seems to me a great shame that we are more interested in the speed with which we can make our meals than the process or the ritual of preparing and enjoying our food. It is a pity when we have so much wonderful fresh produce available to us that we would, for example, buy a polystyrene tray of vegetables encased in plastic, fruit that has sat in a box in a cold-storage fridge for three months or fish which has been frozen and pre-prepared in a cocktail of chemicals.

Certainly, with our lives being so consumed by our work we have had to invent new 'hassle free' ways to put dinner on the table, but it is my feeling that this has come at some cost.

As far as I can see there isn't a great deal of interaction with the person delivering pizza to your door, nor is there any behind the supermarket trolley — it's a case of run down the aisles and grab. It's stand in a queue and flick through a magazine, it's 'let's not communicate'. We sit at home watching one box and eating out of another. Supermarkets are stocking more and more of the goods we used to buy in small shops. They now have fruit and vegetable sections, a deli, butchers and fish sections. And as each of these new sections opens, the doors of a small business close.

At the markets, there is no pre-wrapping. Most of the produce is picked within twenty-four hours of it arriving at the market. It may be blemished, but you can bet it will taste real.

One man I met at the market sold vegetables grown in his backyard. When I rang him later to organise a time to come and see his garden, his wife told me he'd gone fishing. I asked her if she would mind if I came out anyway to look at the garden and she said, 'No, we not got much. No, we got nothing.' To her it seemed so little, but what she was telling me was that her husband sold what they didn't use at home. He ran a stall, not for the money — he often only had a box or so to sell — but because it was a social event for him. He charged only $2.00 a kilo for his produce and I estimated that even if he sold out each week, he could not be making much more than about $50.00. He picked the vegetables himself every morning before the markets. They were fresh and they tasted like vegetables should. Sweet. I hope to pay tribute in this book to this man and the many others like him and to the wonders produced from their gardens of 'not much'.

This cookbook is not for the faint-hearted who won't listen to their instincts or to the spirit of a recipe. The recipes were mostly collected 'live' from market stalls around Australia. They were often told to me by the market stall holders in between selling sacks of potatoes or were muttered over a shoulder while cutting cheese or disclosed bit by bit while sitting on a box and yelling, 'Come on! Nice fresh tomatoes. Two dollars a kilo. Come on, no-one fresher. Picked this morning. Come on, come and get it. Two dollars a kilo...' This book is not about measurements but a way of cooking that requires tasting, testing and imagination.

When I first started talking to people, I was always questioning them. 'Are you sure there are no onions in this recipe? What about herbs, any garlic?' I was surprised how simple many of the recipes were, I thought

I knew a fair bit about Italian cooking until I started writing this book. Until you understand the culture behind the cuisine, you will never really have a feel for the food.

As you read through this book, you will see that it is structured just as it was collected. We haven't divided it into sections based on courses, just by the people who generously shared their culinary delights. To me, this book is not only about food, but about the people to whom these recipes belong.

Many recipes call for salt which, for health reasons, has become a bit of a no-no. Of course it's important to watch your sodium intake, but many of these recipes won't taste as they should unless salt is added, so use it here and try and be sure to balance it by going easy on it in other areas. Also, when salt is called for, always use either rock or sea salt. These kinds of salt are more natural, contain important minerals and have a better flavour which doesn't leave that bitter taste of iodised salt in your mouth.

These are recipes from cultures steeped in history and tradition and I hope their warmth and generosity resonate through these pages. When you make these dishes, picture these people, be generous with your ingredients, use lots of good quality olive oil and enjoy.

Note on spelling

Throughout this book I have spelt oregano — the classic herb of the Mediterranean — in the Italian (origano) and Greek (rigani) ways as so many people who shared their recipes with me still used those forms even when speaking English.

Giovanni Iannelli

Port Adelaide Market

It was early morning at the Port Adelaide markets, my first day on the job and I was nervous. Giovanni was the first person I approached about this book and my heart sank when he said to me across boxes of beans and tomatoes, 'I got nothing to tell you. I do nothing special.' A cloud as dark as the skin of his eggplants gathered above me, and the whole project seemed about to fall from my grasp. Luckily Giovanni's son, who was working the stall with him that morning, overheard our short discussion and prompted his father. 'Go on Dad, tell her about your tomato sauce,' then, turning to me, he said proudly, 'Dad's a really good cook.'

Giovanni finally agreed to tell me some of his culinary specialties. I sat on an empty wooden box as he began to tell me his recipe for homemade tomato sauce in between selling his beans — $2.00 a kilo for the freshest, sweetest beans. The recipe went something like this:

'Okay. Tomato sauce. You don't use cans. You make your own', he said before turning out towards the crowds and yelling, 'Beans $2.00 a kilo. Come on get your beans.' People milled around the stall but he turned back towards me, sitting on the box, and continued. 'Okay, so you get 20 kilos of, you know, fresh tomatoes. Ripe ones $2.00 a kilo, come on fresh beans. Two kilos? Here you are. Thank you. Yes, $4.00.' It was hard to keep track of where we were going. After he finished his sale, I said, 'Giovanni, hang on. Can you tell me using not so many tomatoes?'

'No,' he yelled, this time at me, not out to the crowd. 'You got to use 20 kilos, 'cause you give your sauce to your brother and your sister and your family. You not use any less. More maybe, yes. But no less.' Well, you get the idea and the condensed recipe follows.

Giovanni taught me an invaluable lesson that first morning and to me Giovanni's sauce is the essence of this book. Behind this sauce lies a culture and a way of being far removed from late-twentieth-century living. It is about ritual, caring, sharing and providing.

Giovanni's Homemade Tomato Sauce

20 kg ripe tomatoes — romas are the best for this sauce because they tend to be less juicy and have fewer seeds

fresh basil sprigs

salt

sterilised beer bottles or other sealable sterilised bottles

First, you need to remove the skins from the tomatoes by plunging them into boiling water. Traditionally this is done in a large copper but you can use any large pot. When the skin of the tomatoes cracks, strain and then peel them. Squeeze the seeds out, and add a little salt to taste to the remaining pulp.

Clean the beer or glass soft drink bottles. Sterilise the bottles by boiling them in water for an hour. You will need to buy beer bottle tops from a shop and a special device to secure the tops to the bottles (usually available from shops which supply beer-making ingredients and equipment).

Fill the sterilised bottles with the tomato pulp and add a sprig of fresh basil. Seal the bottles and preserve your sauce by putting them back into the copper and boiling in lots of water for another hour.

Because of the large quantities used by Giovanni, he uses his copper for preserving. Before he puts in the sealed bottles, he lines the copper with layers of sack or old cloth to prevent the glass from cracking while the bottles boil in the preserving process.

The sauce can be stored for up to a year in the bottles and can be used as a sauce just on its own or can become the basis of other tomato-based pasta toppings. For a very simple pasta sauce add oil, more basil and a little salt and pepper to the preserved tomato mixture. Reduce to taste and the right consistency.

Invite friends over for a sauce-bottling day. Drink beautiful wine, make a delicious lunch and at the end of the day everyone will take home with them a few wonderful bottles of homemade tomato sauce. A sauce-making day sure beats lugging home from the supermarket heavy plastic bags, splitting at the seams and cutting into the palms of your hands from the weight of canned whole peeled tomatoes.

Instead of, or as well as, a bottle of wine, take to a friend's dinner a bottle of your own homemade sauce.

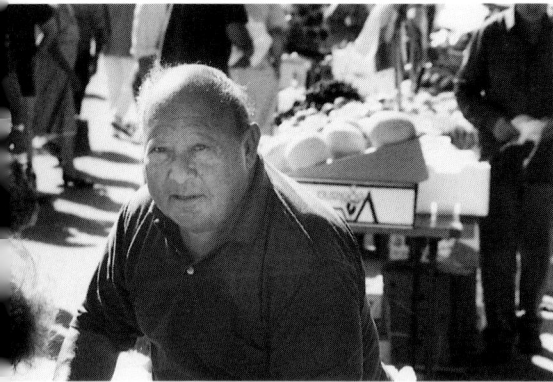

After Giovanni gave me his recipe for tomato sauce, he invited me to his home to see his garden. I was thrilled, this was exactly how I had hoped this project would proceed. I had wanted to make connections between food and gardens, produce and people. Enthusiastically, I arranged a time to call Giovanni at home. When I called, Giovanni's wife answered and told me Giovanni had gone fishing. 'Fine,' I thought running through my schedule, I'd be able to visit him the following day before I drove to Melbourne. I asked his wife if I could come and see them tomorrow.

'No,' she said. 'I said he gone fishing.'

'Yes, yes I know, but I'll come tomorrow.'

'No,' she said emphatically, 'he gone fishing! He gone for four days.'

So Giovanni had gone fishing and I rearranged my plans. I wasn't able to visit, but it all worked out fine because the next time I went to Adelaide I asked him what he had caught on that famous boating expedition and, of course, how he cooked it.

Squid

1 medium-sized squid

1 onion, chopped

garlic, crushed

1 glass white wine

finely chopped Italian parsley

chilli flakes

olive oil

Clean the squid and cut it into small pieces. Put it in a saucepan with no oil and heat through well to remove all the moisture. This method of cooking, where you dry the squid out in the pan first before cooking, keeps the squid a nice colour.

After the moisture has evaporated, add the onion and garlic to the squid and fry them all in a little olive oil. When the onion is transparent, add a glass of wine, throw in a handful of parsley and some chilli (if you like it hot) and heat through before serving.

Stuffed Squid

Giovanni's fishing trip was more of a squid-catching expedition than anything else. As a consequence, Giovanni had to test his culinary abilities by cooking the squid in a different way each night for his fishing companions. Here is another way he cooked these tentacled marine creatures on that fishing trip.

squid tubes

fresh bread, crumbed (enough to absorb moisture from the meat and egg)

lean mince meat or Italian sausage

1 egg, beaten

parmigiano cheese

salt and pepper

Clean the squid. In a bowl, mix the bread which you have made into crumbs with the mince meat or sausage, the beaten egg and the parmigiano cheese. Be sure to use crumbs you have made yourself because the ones you buy from the shops in a box are not appropriate for stuffings as they are too dry. When the ingredients are well combined add salt and pepper to taste. Pack the stuffing tightly into the squid tubes.

Heat olive oil in a saucepan and saute the tubes to seal them. Then turn the heat down, put a lid on the pan and braise so the meat inside the tubes cooks through. Alternatively, you can bake them in a hot oven.

When I made this dish I added chopped parsley and garlic to the stuffing and accompanied it with a fresh green salad. Fresh bread dipped into olive oil is perfect with this dish and the salad.

Until now, I had always thought that when I went to a deli I was right to ask for *a* salami. Now I know that for all these years I have been asking for more than one. I'm sure many an Italian deli owner has been tempted to pull out a number of them for me to buy and that it is from years of experience that they have learned to interpret what we say. In Italian, the *i* generally indicates the plural and the *e* the singular. Hence, in this recipe I have written salame because I mean for you to use only one. So, next time you go with friends to an Italian cafe, be sure when ordering more than one cappuccino to say cappuccini!

Giovanni's String Beans

string beans

tomato sauce (see Giovanni's recipe or
use very ripe fresh tomatoes)

fresh Italian pork sausage or salame

nutmeg

salt and pepper

Fry the sausage in a little olive oil. Add the beans and fry just enough to coat in oil. Add the tomato sauce* and a pinch of nutmeg and salt and pepper to taste. When the beans are cooked through, but still very crisp, take off the stove and serve as an accompaniment to a *secondo*.

*If you are using fresh tomatoes, not already preserved ones, cook them through to reduce the amount of liquid and to soften before adding them to the beans. This procedure will concentrate the flavours and prevent the beans from overcooking.

Peter & Mauro Altamura

Fisherman's Wharf Port Adelaide Market

Of all the markets I visited, the Port Adelaide market is without a doubt my favourite. Its lack of structure, its ad hoc nature, I adore. All the markets have their own special something — for me the Central market in Adelaide is full of happy memories from my adolescence, the Vic markets are new and full of the most wonderful treasures to discover … for me though the Port stands apart from them all. Perhaps it's because it's in the middle of nowhere, sitting at the end of the acres and acres of wasteland where Adelaide's supposed saviour, the Multi-Function Polis, was to be situated. The irony that the site for Australia's proposed Silicon Valley is actually the driveway to what is perhaps Australia's least glamorous market is a wonderful twist.

To get to the market you must drive through the suburb of Port Adelaide, which is in itself a wonderful place to visit. Old sandstone cottages and shops with wide verandahs line the streets.

The Port market is a maverick and I think above all that's what I love about it. Confirming this story was hard, but it was told to me by so many people that I have assumed it to be true. Some years ago there was a dispute at the markets in town (at that time there were two markets — Central and the East End markets). Many of the growers felt they were being shut out by the bigger suppliers and found themselves with produce rotting on their vines, unable to find buyers. After a period of disputation, a group of growers decided to start their own market and so the Port Adelaide market was born. It's a rebellious market, it's a 'we won't be stopped' market and it still has that feel about it, even after all these years.

Sitting out there in the middle of nowhere it has survived and the people who sell their produce there have been able to maintain their livelihood and a rich tradition.

Peter, Mauro and their brothers work together on their small fishing boat. Every Sunday morning you can find them moored to the wharf at the Port Adelaide market with a boatload of fish, caught during the night. They sell only what they catch, so you can never be sure exactly what you'll be able to buy from them but usually they will have an array of fish like snook, garfish and tommy ruffs. Using a set of scales they erect in the middle of the boat, they will sell you wonderfully fresh fish by the kilo at fantastically cheap prices.

When I listened to the tape I recorded with Mauro, I could hardly hear him over the yelling of his brothers. 'Tommys, come on $2.00 ... come on, I sell you all the rest [about 5 kg if I remember correctly] for ... $5.00. Come on, we wanna go home now, all the lot $5.00.' Then they made jokes at Mauro, invited me to go out fishing with them one night and gave me these wonderful recipes. Mauro and Peter eat the soup recipe after their fishing expeditions and I can see why — it's homely and warming and I can picture their strong fishing hands soaking chunks of bread in large bowls of steaming soup.

The boat is always full. Not only with the Altamura brothers, but with their friends too, all of whom seem to enjoy getting into the spirit of yelling and selling. The wharf they moor at, along with all the other boats, is only small and somehow the boys managed to get themselves the mooring closest to the markets so it's the Altamura brothers who'll yell their prices at you first. Something tells me they charmed themselves there.

Unlike some of the fishermen at the wharf who also sell filleted fish, Mauro and his brothers only sell whole fish. Italians will tell you this is the only way to buy fish. Even if a recipe calls for fillets, use the bones and the head left over from the filleting to make a fresh fish stock for a soup which, with added vegetables and pasta, can be served as the *primo* (first course) of any meal.

Wrapped Garfish

Mauro and Peter love this dish. Freshly filleted garfish fillets wrapped in dough are a traditional peasant twist to the pizza.

For the dough:

25 g fresh yeast

4 cups plain flour

1 tablespoon olive oil

warm water

1 teaspoon salt

To make the dough, dissolve the yeast in a little of the warm water, then pour in the oil, add the salt and stir until dissolved.

Put the flour in a mixing bowl and make a well in the middle. Add the yeast mixture and mix gently. Gradually add more of the warm water while you mix until you have a stiff bread-like dough.

Take the dough out of the bowl and, on a lightly floured clean dry surface, knead the dough until it is smooth and elastic. This should take about 10 minutes. When it is ready, put the dough into an oiled clean bowl and cover with a tea-towel. Let stand in a warm place for about 45 minutes.

Filling:

6 garfish fillets

butter

olive oil

1 onion, chopped

1 kg fresh ripe tomatoes, chopped

While the dough is rising, fillet the garfish and fry it in a little butter and oil. Put aside. Fry the onion together with the tomatoes in a little olive oil.

When dough is ready, divide it equally so each fillet will have its own case. Roll out the dough segments on a lightly floured clean surface with a rolling pin you have wiped with olive oil. Put a piece of fish on top of each piece of dough, then add a little of the tomato and onion mixture to the top of each piece of fish. Fold the dough over the fish like a pasty and press the edges together so it is sealed. Bake in a hot oven (180°C) until the dough is cooked through.

Fish soup is a very traditional dish in so far as it uses the same basic ingredients to create both the *primo* and *secondo* courses. The liquid formed as you cook the fish becomes the sauce for the pasta served as the first course and the fish itself makes up the *secondo* (main or second course). Both courses need to be eaten hot, so keep some of the sauce aside to heat the fish.

When Mauro gave me this recipe I kept trying to remind him of ingredients I thought he had forgotten. Every time I suggested he may have left out something vital, such as garlic or basil, he would shake his head with some disdain. 'No, you keep it simple. This is how we make it at home,' he said, quoting back my own brief to him. Simplicity and the courage to let flavours stand on their own are intregal parts of Italian cuisine.

Fish Soup

1 kg fresh ripe tomatoes, chopped

2 large onions, chopped

olive oil

a whole (gutted and scaled) fresh firm-fleshed fish or fillets (snapper or snook)

spaghetti

salt and pepper to taste

Cook tomatoes and onions in olive oil slowly for about an hour. Add water if the mixture starts to dry out. Remember this liquid will become a rich sauce, so take care not to make it too watery or it will lose its flavour — it should be quite thick.

Just before the sauce is ready, cook some spaghetti in salted boiling water until al dente.

A few minutes before the pasta is ready to drain, add the fish to the tomato and onion sauce. If you use the whole fish, cook for about 3 minutes until the meat comes off the bone. If you use the fillets, cook for a slightly shorter period of time until the fish is cooked through but not falling apart. The fillets should stay together so they can be served individually.

Remove the fish from the sauce and put aside to serve as the *secondo*. Don't forget to save a little of the sauce to serve with the fish to keep it moist. Pour the sauce on the pasta and serve in individual bowls with a drizzle of olive oil on top. Reheat the fish gently (if necessary) and serve with a *contorno* (side dish) of your choice. Usually a green salad and bread will be sufficient.

Antonietta & Emilio Vairo

Victoria Markets

Antonietta and Emilio run the cake store at the Vic markets. There were too many distractions at the shop, so they invited me to their home where we could talk without interruption. Emilio was keen to show me his garden which he was very proud of. Antonietta said there wasn't a lot to see, but I wasn't swayed because I knew it would probably be fantastic and she was more than likely being modest.

It was indeed a great garden. They grew artichokes, fresh broad beans which we peeled and ate as we walked around, many trees heavy with sweet fruits and one or two olive trees.

It was everything and more that I had hoped for. Jack played football with their son Frank and his daughter while I inspected the garden, then we all went inside and talked cooking.

As we sat down at their table, Frank turned to me and said, 'Mum's a great cook,' and we were off. Emilio told us about making cheese when he was a boy growing up in Naples. In the south there were lots of farms for grazing and the cheese made from the milk of the animals, he said, was just wonderful. Unfortunately, the temperature here isn't conducive to making cheese, although Emilio and Antonietta did try it a few times when they first arrived in Australia before deciding it was easier to buy it than to make. In Italy, Emilio milked the sheep, taking the milk in a big pail to his mother who would warm it on the fire and add to it some old milk that had gone off. The old milk was full of natural yeast and it would ferment the fresh batch. When it was a ricotta-like consistency, it was hung up in cloth so the water seeped out, then salted, put in a round container, covered and left for six months in a cool dry place.

Antonietta described the fire they cooked on in the house and how her parents smoked a pig so it was preserved for the whole year by hanging it next to the heat. Frank looked at his mother and started laughing, visualising, I guess, his mother's family all huddled around the fire, with a pig hanging on a hook beside them. Jack asked, 'You hung the pig in the kitchen?' with an element of shock in his voice and we all cracked up.

Frank told me about his Dad's favourite dish which is incredibly simple and hearty.

Hearty Beef Stew

1 onion

garlic, crushed

big chunks of meat (some pieces
still with the bone)

1 bottle homemade tomato sauce
(see Giovanni's recipe, page 4)

olive oil

Fry the onion and the garlic in the oil until transparent. Add the chunks of meat and stir to brown. Add the bottle of homemade tomato sauce and cook on a low heat for about an hour, adding water if the mixture gets too dry.

Cook pasta in lots of salted boiling water. Pour the sauce the meat was cooked in over the pasta and serve as a *primo*, then serve the meat as a *secondo* with crusty bread and side vegetables.

It was getting late and we needed to get home, but before we left, we all went back out to the garden and Jack and I were given bags and bags of fresh fruit and vegetables to take with us.

As they picked vegetables from their garden I said how surprised I was at the simplicity of many of the recipes I had been given and how I had been fooled into believing all these years that Italian food always needed lots of different herbs and tonnes of garlic.

Emilio looked up from the bush he was searching for artichokes to give us and said, 'Caro, if you put too much, you lose the flavour.' It's a simple lesson, but I now have it often in my mind when I cook. The following dish of Antonietta's is a perfect example of that maxim.

Antonietta's Cannellini Beans with Tomato

½ kg cannellini beans

1 bottle homemade tomato sauce (see page 4)

salt

olive oil

Soak the cannellini beans in cold water overnight. Discard the water and drain the beans well. Pour them back in the pot and cover with cold water, then place on the stove and cook for about an hour until tender.

When soft, drain the water and pour in a bottle of fresh tomato sauce, add salt and heat through while stirring.

When hot, serve the beans drizzled with lots of olive oil on crusty bread.

'At home when it was cold, we used to call this a good meal. We had it with some cheese and some wine and, especially in winter, it was good,' explained Emilio with a look on his face that told me he would cook this dish up the first moment he could.

Frank had just explained how nothing of a pig goes to waste in Italy, which prompted this recipe from his Dad. Emilio says he prefers pigs' liver to that of other beasts because he thinks it tastes a lot sweeter, but if you can't get pigs', most other kinds of liver can be cooked in this way.

Emilio's Fegato di Maya

4 pigs' livers, cleaned

3 rashers bacon

olive oil

whole chillis

lemon wedges for juice

Chop the livers and the bacon into small slices. Heat the olive oil in a saucepan and add the bacon. Cook through then add the livers and the chilli. The livers shouldn't be cooked too long or they will dry out and lose their appeal. They should be cooked through but still pink in the centre.

Serve with fresh crusty bread dipped in olive oil, and lemon wedges on the side to squeeze over the liver. Accompany with a salad.

Another way to cook the liver is to marinate it for at least an hour in some olive oil and lemon juice. Grill the liver under a hot flame while basting with the marinade.

Again this is perfect served with bread dipped in oil. Squeeze fresh lemon juice over the liver and accompany with a salad.

the GRiLLi Family

Vignerons and olive oil producers,
Virginia, South Australia

The Grilli family has been making wine for many years. 'It's in my blood,' says Joseph, the eldest son who has taken over much of the responsibility of the business. The inspiration to make olive oil came to Joseph after he and his wife, Dina, visited Tuscany, where they saw other small wineries similar to theirs producing exquisite olive oils.

When they returned to Australia they set about learning the differences between olives, the various oil contents of different kinds of olives and the process of producing quality extra virgin olive oil. 'It works well with the grapes because after we finish the wine season we have a short break and then move straight into the olive oil season. Olive picking starts in May, but really gets going by June and July when the olives are at their plumpest,' Joseph explains.

Joseph has made one of the best oils I have ever tasted — its rich taste and wonderful aroma is hard to get past — and I asked him how he had learned and mastered this old tradition.

'Making olive oil is similar to making wine and that's why I understand it. With the wine, it matters when you pick the fruit, and it's the same for the olives. How quickly you press after picking is crucial in both processes, so you can see it's very similar. I'm pretty convinced that as long as you have fresh olives you can make good oil,' he said. But, Joe explains, the making of oil is not something he taught himself although he has perfected the technique. 'I was lucky enough to know the guy who'd been picking the olives in the foothills for thirty-five years. He and others taught me a lot. Until recently the oil was only ever made for personal use though, so it was done in a pretty rustic way. It still is made as it was then, but we try and take a bit more care and we're trying to import new kinds of olives from Italy that are better for olive oil production.'

It was a very hot day in Adelaide when Joe enthusiastically met with me to talk olives, on his only day off. After he had explained the olive oil making process to me over a good strong brew of coffee, he said, 'Come on, you've got to see this.' We got in his car and drove up to the Adelaide foothills so I could experience the magic of olives myself. This grove, ten minutes from town, tucked into the hills and surrounded by houses, is incredibly beautiful. I felt like I was walking into a sacred place. Quiet and full of history. The grove was planted in the mid-1800s and is one of only a few still left standing that were planted by the same man over a century ago.

We walked in the heat through the rows of gnarled old trees and Joe looked a little disappointed. 'It's not going to be a good year,' he said. 'Not enough rain. Look at these. Usually these should be double the size by now. Not enough rain,' he said again, shaking his head.

Joe is faced with the continual problem of demand outstripping production yet he is happy to be part of what, in Australia, is still a very new industry. 'I'm planting trees myself, but it will be a long time before they yield in any substantial way. It takes eight to ten years before a tree fully matures, but in the meantime I'm buying olives from the people I know and making sure they get on the press quickly so the quality is fantastic.'

Joe talks with such enthusiasm it's not hard to see why he has mastered the art of oil. He loves the process and the culture behind it, which is after all his own.

Strictly speaking, the Grilli family should fall outside the boundaries of this book which is meant only to include the recipes of those people who work at markets. However, I have included them along with Maria and Rosalinda from Victoria (page 167) because, although once removed, they are still very much connected to the markets. If the market place itself is the heart of this book, then these are the veins supplying the produce that makes the heart beat.

Joe worked with his family on these recipes, all of which particularly feature the wonderful flavour of good quality olive oil. I suggest you go out and buy a bottle of Joseph's oil to really immerse yourself in the spirit of the Mediterranean.

Joe and Dina Grilli use this recipe at home to show off their olive oil. They say it is especially good with globe artichokes which have been boiled until tender in lightly salted water. Once cooked, the leaves, tender flesh, heart and stem of the artichoke are all dipped into the pinzimonio. You can also serve pinzimonio drizzled over, or in a bowl beside, a selection of fresh raw vegetables such as fennel, celery, radicchio, carrot, radish and mushrooms.

Pinzimonio

(Olive Oil Dip)

$^{3}/_{4}$ cup olive oil

$^{1}/_{4}$ cup red wine vinegar

sea salt

garlic cloves, crushed

freshly ground black pepper

Steep crushed garlic in olive oil for about an hour. Remove garlic. Add vinegar, salt and pepper to taste. Mix well until the oil and vinegar are combined and serve as suggested above.

Dina's salad recipe reminds me of Caesar salad, but I prefer this idea: salty with anchovies, crisp and bitter with fresh salad greens, balanced with the oil and vinegar then softened by the cheese, it has the full spectrum of tastes, textures and flavours.

Pancetta Salad

½ yellow capsicum, sliced thinly

2 ripe tomatoes, cut into small pieces

8 anchovy fillets, cut into small pieces

¾ cup shaved parmigiano

10 thin slices pancetta, cut into quarters

olive oil

red wine vinegar

pepper

a large bowl of washed and drained mixed salad greens (make sure your mix has bitter greens like radicchio and rocket)

Fry the pancetta in a small amount of oil until crispy. Place lettuce, capsicum, tomatoes, anchovies and parmigiano in a large bowl. Add cooked pancetta while still hot and about ⅓ of a cup of olive oil.

Warm up about 4–5 tablespoons of vinegar in the same pan so the vinegar will take on some of the pancetta's flavour. Allow to cool and pour the vinegar over the salad. Add freshly ground pepper to taste and toss well.

The salad is now ready to serve and can be eaten as is, or with fresh crusty bread.

Italians never waste any meat and to do so would be an obscene luxury. This recipe uses rich chicken livers to make a superb pâté, not as heavy as the French version which has cream. The saltiness of the anchovies and the tartness of the capers make this a really unusual pâté that I, like Joe and Dina, just couldn't get enough of.

Joseph and Dina discovered this pâté when they stayed in the picturesque hilltop town of Collazzone in Umbria in 1992. They bought it from the village's small local deli and found themselves back there almost daily to replenish their supply of this wonderful Umbrian spread. When they left the village, they asked the deli owner for the recipe so they could make it at home.

Umbrian Pâté

1 medium onion, diced

5 chicken livers, cleaned thoroughly
and roughly chopped

6 sage leaves

7 anchovy fillets in oil

2 tablespoons of capers in vinegar

salt and pepper to taste

white wine

olive oil

Fry onion in a little olive oil until transparent. Add chicken livers and brown quickly. Turn down heat. Add sage leaves, anchovies, capers, a splash of wine if the mixture is dry and salt and pepper to taste. Remember not to add too much salt because the anchovies and the capers are very salty. Cook on low heat until livers are cooked (5–10 minutes). Puree the mixture. Drizzle in some olive oil to make a smooth paste.

Serve with fresh crusty Italian bread.

Italian cuisine is famous for vegetables filled with lean meats, rice, cheese and herbs. Stuffing vegetables like capsicum successfully turns them into a meal in themselves. Here is a slight variation on the theme of stuffing and another use for that wonderful Italian loaf. Here too, a mere loaf is turned almost into a whole meal. This is the perfect picnic dish, prepared the night before, easy to carry and full of fabulous flavours.

Pagnotta Ripieno

1 large round Italian white bread loaf with a not too crunchy crust
(if you use a softer crust bread it will be easier to cut for serving)

1 can artichokes in brine or preserved in oil, shredded

$\frac{1}{2}$ red capsicum, diced finely

2 garlic cloves, crushed

$\frac{1}{2}$ jar green stuffed olives

2 tablespoons capers, chopped

4 tablespoons dried tomatoes or capsicums, shredded

handful of Italian parsley, finely chopped

black pepper

olive oil

thinly sliced sopressa, mortadella, prosciutto

mild cheese such as mozzarella or bocconcini, sliced

ripe tomatoes, sliced

Cut the top off the loaf and keep aside as the lid. Scoop out some bread from inside the loaf and the lid, but be sure to leave the sides and bottom thick enough for the stuffing to stay safely inside the casing. Brush base, sides and lid of the bread with a good amount of olive oil.

In a bowl, make a salad with the artichokes, capsicum, olives, capers, dried tomatoes, parsley, garlic, pepper and olive oil. Let stand for at least 1 hour (the longer the better).

Make layers in the loaf starting with half the salad, then the sopressa, mortadella, tomato, cheese, prosciutto and finally the remaining salad. Place the lid back on top of the loaf. Wrap the loaf tightly in foil and place in the refrigerator overnight, weighed down with a heavy object.

Overnight, the flavours will mingle and the layers will compact so the loaf can be easily sliced in wedges to serve.

Panzanella

Many traditional Italian recipes are incredibly simple. The ingredients are few, but the flavours, when put together, are simply wonderful. Joseph's face lights up as he describes this dish his mother, Santina Grilli, brings out to the family for breakfast in the vineyard during grape picking.

Rub garlic onto slices of crusty bread. Sprinkle with red wine vinegar. Drizzle with olive oil and sprinkle with freshly ground black pepper and salt.

One of my friends remembers eating a variation of this recipe in Pavia. Almost daily she enjoyed warm bread straight from the baker's oven which had been sprinkled with origano and a few chilli flakes and then drenched in virgin olive oil.

This is another dish perfect for summer picnics when the oranges are sweet and ripe. Much Italian cooking is about balance and I often wonder just how some of the combinations were first brought together. In this simple salad the strong aniseed taste of the fennel is perfectly pitted against the sweetness of fresh oranges and then carefully counterbalanced with the savoury olives.

Fennel and Orange Salad

3 oranges

1 bulb of fennel

a handful of ripe black olives

extra virgin olive oil

red wine vinegar

salt and pepper

Peel oranges and cut into round slices. Cut the fennel into thin wedges. Place in a salad bowl with the olives. Dress with the olive oil and good quality red wine vinegar (or your favourite type of vinegar), salt and pepper.

In some parts of Italy this salad isn't made with the vinegar, the idea being that the acidity of the oranges is strong enough to balance the fennel. Often, it is served with finely chopped Italian parsley as well.

Italians are wonderful culinary recyclers. Traditionally, nothing goes to waste which is why there is such a lot of pickling and preserving in Italian kitchens. What couldn't be eaten at the time of harvest was pickled or preserved to last until it was needed.

In Italy, loaves of bread are baked or bought throughout the day, so with every meal a fresh loaf is served, often still warm from the oven. It seems only natural then, that a recipe was invented to make use of the many not quite fresh loaves of bread that accumulate in Italian households.

The day before you intend making this dish, choose a loaf of white Italian bread, or else ask your baker to sell you a loaf of yesterday's bread. Ideally though, you will keep true to tradition and already have in the house a loaf which is too good for toast (or, if you are Italian, to dry in the oven to have with coffee and milk for breakfast), but not quite fresh enough for bread and cheese.

This peasant dish makes good use of stale bread and an abundance of ripe tomatoes, along with basil and, of course, best quality Joseph olive oil. Pappa al pomodoro transforms stale bread into something more than wonderful.

Pappa al Pomodoro

1/2 cup extra virgin olive oil

3 cloves garlic, chopped

1/2 cup fresh basil leaves

250 g stale continental bread, sliced thinly

8 cups homemade chicken stock

1 kg peeled, seeded and chopped ripe tomatoes

In a saucepan, saute garlic in oil. Add bread slices and brown lightly on both sides. Add tomatoes and cook for a few minutes on high heat, stirring well with a wooden spoon. Then add chicken stock and basil and simmer with the lid on over a low heat for about 20 minutes. Taste for seasoning, turn off heat and let rest for about an hour. Reheat and serve in bowls drizzled with plenty of olive oil.

This is a traditional Italian way to cook a whole snook, but any other firm-fleshed whole fish such as bream or snapper tastes equally good cooked this way. I love the basting method for its theatrics, but as is usually the case with Italian cooking, there is a very good reason for the drama.

BBQ Snook

1 whole snook, gutted and scaled

bay leaves

garlic cloves, sliced

lemon slices and juice of 1 lemon

Joseph olive oil

salt and pepper

sprigs of fresh origano or rosemary

With a sharp knife, cut three diagonal slits into each side of the fish. Place a bay leaf, a slice of lemon and some garlic in each slit. Sprinkle fish with salt, squeeze over the lemon juice and drizzle the olive oil over the fish. Let marinate for at least 1 hour before placing on a hot barbecue (a charcoal or wood-fired oven gives the best flavour but barbecuing the fish is just as good).

Dip sprigs of fresh origano or rosemary in a mixture of olive oil, lemon juice and garlic and use like a brush to baste the fish while it cooks. This basting method means the flavour of the rosemary or origano will touch the fish without dominating its delicate taste.

Talking to first-generation Italian–Australians about their cuisine taught me many things but perhaps the best lesson, which can be applied across the board in Italian cooking, is that simplicity is often the key ingredient. This recipe from Joe's mother, Santina, who came from Italy with her parents in the 1950s, is incredibly simple and it is a dish I especially enjoy when I'm sick with a cold or the flu — the oil and garlic are remedy for any fever. Although Joe's parents, Santina and Primo, were born in the same small village, they only met here in Australia.

Spaghetti A'll Aglio E Olio

500 g spaghetti

3 large cloves garlic, crushed

150 ml olive oil

salt and pepper to taste

Cook spaghetti in plenty of boiling salted water to which you have added a dash of olive oil. Heat the olive oil with the garlic but do not let the garlic brown, just warm it gently. When the spaghetti is cooked, drain it well and transfer to a serving bowl. Pour in the oil and garlic and toss well.

There are many variations of this recipe. Some of the people I spoke with used finely chopped flat Italian parsley which they added to the pan of oil and garlic, just long enough to warm through, not cook. Others chopped fresh chillis which they added along with the parsley for a spicy alternative.

Silvana Zamberlan

These recipes from Dina's mother, Silvana Zamberlan, are from Treviso in the Veneto (Venice) region of Italy. It is said that Venetians, whose history is steeped in the waters of their romantic city, like their food to remind them of their home. So expect these recipes to be rich and moist.

It was just over one hundred years ago that Italy became a unified country so it is not surprising that most Italians strongly identify with their province. Often when I asked people at the markets where they were from, they would name only their province and not mention Italy at all. In many Italians' minds, it is as though the country is still divided and there is great allegiance to the province of birth. Italy is a country steeped in history and different dialects are still spoken throughout the various regions. As with differences in language, there are different culinary methods and styles in each province. These differences often relate to the geography of the region — for example, Naples became the centre for pasta because of its excellent durum wheat. It is also a city blessed with perfect conditions for pasta making. The warm winds blowing from Vesuvius coupled with the cool breezes from the coast mean the pasta dries out, but not so quickly that the dough can't be kneaded.

It is quite common in Italy for there to be many slight variations of a single recipe. For example, in the south, recipes may strongly feature one particular ingredient. In the north you may find similar recipes that differ only in one ingredient, but one which alters the end result quite considerably. These slight but significant variations can be traced back to the availability of ingredients depending on the climate and conditions (both geographic and, of course, economic) of the region.

Biscotto

wood-fired oven baked bread

3 roughly chopped ripe tomatoes

½ large Spanish onion, roughly chopped

olive oil

fresh origano or basil leaves

salt and pepper

Place the tomatoes and the Spanish onion in a small bowl. Pour a good amount of olive oil over the mixture. Add freshly ground black pepper and salt. Mix in the fresh herb leaves and let stand for at least an hour.

On a platter arrange the bread that has been roughly broken into bite-sized pieces. Pour a bit of olive oil over the bread pieces, then spoon on the tomato salad and serve.

Silvana loves olive oil, and this recipe and the others she gave me are ideal for her and her family of dedicated oil lovers.

Silvana adds a few drops of olive oil to a bowl of hot broth or minestrone and this is a suggestion that once you've tried, you'll never abandon. The difference a drizzle of oil makes is quite fantastic and, because it's not cooked with any of the other ingredients, just added later, the strong olive taste really permeates the soup.

Silvana also pours olive oil over char-grilled fish, then she sprinkles it with a little balsamic vinegar or lemon juice which brings out the flavour of the flesh.

Bigoli in Salsa

Bigoli is the name of a large type of spaghetti which you will find at any good deli. This is a traditional Veneto dish which is often served on Good Friday for lunch when Catholics do not eat any meat. Dina says this is one of her favourite dishes.

500 g Bigoli spaghetti

4 large onions, sliced thinly

20 anchovy fillets (small Italian variety)

white wine

freshly ground pepper

olive oil

Heat some olive oil in a large frypan, add onions and cook gently until soft. Add anchovy fillets and stir until they break up. Add some pepper to taste and some white wine if the mixture is too dry. Cook pasta in plenty of salted boiling water until al dente*. Drain well. Return to the pan and mix with the sauce. Add more olive oil if the pasta is too dry. This is meant to be an oily dish, so don't be scared to make it that way. With good quality olive oil, you can never go wrong because the taste is so fantastic.

Serve hot, with lots of parmigiano and crusty fresh bread.

*Al dente actually means 'to the tooth', that is, it is cooked to your pleasing. However, correctly cooked pasta shouldn't be too soft so the translation of al dente has come to mean cooked-through but still firm.

There are a number of methods used to test whether your pasta is cooked. A friend of mine bites a long piece of spaghetti in half and then looks into the centre. If the spaghetti isn't cooked properly you will see at the very core of the strand that the flour actually looks uncooked and is a different colour and consistency to the outer layer.

I quite like the dramatics of the testing method where you throw a few strands of pasta at the wall. If they cling to the wall they are cooked, if they fall to the floor, then they require a little longer on the stove.

This is a traditional way to cook game birds. Silvana often served this dish on Easter Sunday and Dina told me that her mother would cook her hand-reared pigeons this way as well — fantastic!

Quaglie in Umido

6 quail

6 slices of pancetta or bacon

sage leaves

rosemary leaves

garlic, slivered

chicken stock

white wine

salt and pepper

olive oil

Clean quail. Pat dry to remove excess moisture. Into each quail place a slice of pancetta, a few sage leaves, a small sprig of rosemary and a tiny sliver of garlic. Heat some oil in a large frying pan. Brown quail all over quickly. Add salt and pepper to taste. Add some extra sage and rosemary leaves and some white wine. Place on lid and turn heat down to low. Cook slowly. Add white wine and/or homemade stock or water as needed. Cook until well done.

Serve the quail with the sauce, accompanied by a radicchio salad and some grilled polenta.

As with much Italian cooking, muset (cotechino) con radicchio e fagioli is served as two courses. The first uses the broth produced while cooking the Cotechino as the basis of a minestrone, and the second course features the Cotechino, accompanied by salad.

This is very much a peasant dish from in and around the province of Treviso. The use of beans with meat features in Italian and other forms of peasant cooking because it was a means of padding out the protein from the scarce and expensive meat which could be used only in small quantities.

Dina says Silvana made this dish often for her when she was growing up and declares that it will 'always remind me of salami season and winter'. Traditionally, salami are made at the beginning of winter — that they could be preserved ensured a supply of protein throughout the cold winter months. Salami making is a wonderful ritual in Italy and it is still practised by Italians here in Australia. When I spoke to Giuseppe Bagnato, the man who crushes olives for the Grilli family's extraordinary olive oil, he described what happens when salami season hits Virginia, a suburb on the outskirts of Adelaide.

Salami season coincides with the months of olive oil production. On a special weekend (usually late in April or early in May), everyone from around the area will come to Giuseppe's huge barn where the olives are crushed. At the height of the season, the presses are working twenty-four hours a day and there are always lots of people around to press the olives while they are still fresh from the trees. On this special weekend, someone will kill one of their pigs and bring it to the shed. It is hung up on a rack, ready to be shared amongst the people. No part of the pig goes to waste. The best meat is cut from the beast and used there and then on the barbecue. Giuseppe told me that one year the kids were so enthusiastic about the whole event that they got carried away and cut the pig up so it wasn't of any use for making salami, it all had to be cooked then and there on the barbecue. Traditionally though, more care is taken and the intestines are saved to encase the salami meat. Everyone from the community takes part in this event and they all take home with them their winter supply of superb salami made exactly to their liking.

From little kids to grandparents, everyone has a role to play in the production of salami — so it is no wonder it is an event that stays so strongly in Dina's mind. Giuseppe said it is a 'good weekend' in a manner that told me that for him, too, it was a pretty special occasion.

I asked Giuseppe about blood pudding which is a very traditional dish. Blood pudding goes to show just how inventive Italians are when it comes to the old proverb, 'Waste not, want not'. Blood pudding is like a salami and is a real delicacy for some. The difference between it and salami is that blood pudding is made, not with meat, but with the blood from the slaughtered pig. Temperature is all important when making blood pudding, because if it's too hot the blood won't congeal and the pudding will be too soft to slice. Some people love blood pudding, but Giuseppe squirmed a little and said they do still make it when they prepare their salami, 'but not very much. I don't like it much. But you know, we keep the tradition so we have a bit,' he said.

It's quite hard for an outsider to become acquainted with the intricacies of old traditions like making blood pudding. I wondered if it had become a secret shared jealously within the Italian community. For so many years first-generation European migrants were seen as strange outsiders and they struggled to be accepted in an often not very welcoming culture. Trying to fit in became a priority and many of their wonderful old traditions have been almost lost in the name of 'getting along'.

The salami made by Giuseppe and his wife are wonderful and he invited me in to his wife's kitchen to explain the process and let me try some for myself. I sat down at their table and they brought out slices of fresh bread, a little bowl of wonderful olive oil poured from a flagon, their own preserved olives and, of course, an array of their special salami. Giuseppe explained that the meat from the pig is minced by hand and mixed with garlic, wild fennel seeds (that you can get from wild fennel plants that you often see growing on the side of the road), salt, lemon peel, chillis and, in the case of the Bagnato family salami, minced red capsicum. The capsicum is mixed with the other ingredients to give the salami a wonderful deep rich red colour. Once the meat is packed into the casings, it is hung up to dry and then the salami are stored under oil which keeps them fresh and moist for the whole of winter. (This isn't a recipe for salami, only an idea of how it's made, so don't try creating your own from here. Buy good quality salami from a deli — these 'directions' are included for colour, not accuracy.)

So back to our recipe after that long explanation of why this dish will always remind Dina of that very special time of year — salami season.

Muset (Cotechino) con Radicchio e Fagioli

1 muset

2 cups dried borlotti beans (soaked in cold water overnight)

2 onions, diced

2 carrots, chopped

3 potatoes, peeled and chopped

1 cup fresh peas

1 cup chopped celery

1 bay leaf

1 tablespoon tomato paste

For serving:

parmigiano, grated

olive oil

fresh horseradish

radicchio and rocket salad

vinegar

Place muset in a large pan. Add enough water to cover. Boil until well-cooked (1–2 hours). To test, pierce with a fork. If the fork is easily removed, the muset is ready. Remove from water and remove skin immediately.

Skim fat off water. This is best done if left overnight to settle. Add 2 cups of dried borlotti beans that have been soaked overnight. Add 'soup' vegetables that have been sauteed in olive oil first. Sauteeing the vegetables before adding them to the water will release their natural sugars and give the dish a subtle sweetness. Traditionally the vegetables used would be carrots, onions, potatoes, peas and celery. Add a bay leaf and a little tomato paste to taste and colour.

Simmer for at least 1½ hours until the vegetables and the beans are cooked. Add salt and pepper to taste. Take out the cooked beans which should have mainly settled at the bottom of the pan. Mash lightly to a thick custard-like consistency. Puree the rest and serve as a vegetable soup — minestrone con i fagioli. Serve very hot and to each bowl add grated parmigiano and a drizzling of olive oil.

Serve the warm muset thickly sliced with horseradish and a radicchio, arugula (rocket) and onion salad. The mashed beans (room temperature) are placed on top of the salad on individual plates. A few drops of oil and vinegar are then added on top of the beans.

If cotechino isn't available a large pork hock can be used instead.

Ezmaralda Simonis

F&S Fruiterers, Prahran Markets,
Melbourne

Prahran is a busy Melbourne suburb, lucky to have these markets since most suburban markets have been lost to large supermarket complexes. Prahran markets have been going for many years, and some of the stall owners I spoke to had been working there for over fifty years.

Ezmaralda works on F&S Fruiterers stall at Prahran markets. Theirs is a stall which has a vast array of both fruit and vegetables.

I talked to Ezmaralda during her lunch break, sitting on boxes of fruit while she ate stuffed peppers from a lunchbox. They looked great even served in a plastic container.

Stuffed Peppers

This recipe includes some mince meat, but as we spoke
just before Easter when Catholics don't eat meat, Ezmaralda
explained that it can also be made without the mince.

6 whole capsicums (depending on size)

½ kilo mince meat

3 onions, chopped in small pieces

parsley, finely chopped

3 fresh ripe tomatoes, chopped

2 cups rice

garlic, crushed

salt and pepper

Cut open the capsicums at the top, just enough to be able to remove the
seeds inside without completely segmenting them. The tops act as lids,
so shouldn't be completely cut through. Remove all the pips and wash
the capsicum.

In a frying pan, saute the onions in olive oil on a low heat for about
5 minutes. Add the chopped parsley, the tomatoes, the garlic and salt
and pepper to taste. Cook for about 5 minutes before adding the mince
meat and the rice. Saute for a few more minutes to cover the mince and
rice in the other ingredients.

Carefully pack the stuffing tightly into the capsicums. Close the lids of
the capsicums over the stuffing. If you accidentally cut off the tops, push
them down firmly over the stuffing, where they should sit securely. Put
the capsicums in a baking dish with 2–3 cups of water depending on the
size of the dish. Bake in a moderate oven for 30 minutes then turn each
capsicum over and bake again until the rice is cooked. If the water in the
dish is low, add a little more. Usually, to cook the second side will take a
further 30 minutes.

Economic realities always impact on culinary culture. Poverty and lack of grazing pastures in Greece meant that meat was scarce and therefore usually only available to the rich in any quantity. So the typical Greek family would have to make meat go a long way. As a result, Greeks, like Italians, use meat sparingly and rarely eat a main course with meat as the feature.

Having said that though, here is a recipe for a leg of lamb stuffed with garlic and served with potatoes. The leg is cooked very slowly for about 3 hours so be sure to put it on in plenty of time for dinner.

Garlic Leg of Lamb

1 leg of lamb

potatoes

garlic

salt and pepper

Cut all the fat from the meat. Slice the garlic into slivers and then make incisions into the meat with a sharp knife. Into each slit, pack a sliver of garlic. Grind sea salt and fresh pepper over the leg.

Put the lamb into a baking tray, preferably a thick ceramic one, into which you put a few cups of water. The water will keep the meat moist while it cooks slowly. Do not put a lid or any foil over the dish and cook it very slowly in the oven for about 2 hours.

Then, peel the potatoes and cut them in halves or keep whole if they are only small. Put them in with the meat, top up the water level in the bottom of the dish if necessary and return it to the oven for another hour. When the potatoes are soft, the dish is ready and is served with a gravy made by reducing the juices in the pan. To make the gravy, don't add any cornflour or thickener, just put the pan on a high heat on the stove until the juices become thick.

Let the meat sit for at least 5 minutes before carving. Serve with the gravy poured over the slices of lamb and accompany with side vegetables of your choice.

Liliana Del Col

Con's Deli, Central Market, Adelaide

My friend Marisa told me about Liliana whom she had known when she was a girl and Liliana worked for her father in his tailor shop in Adelaide. When I wandered through Con's deli, I could see Liliana was very busy, preparing for the rush that was a typical Thursday afternoon at Adelaide Central. Con's deli is very big and it's in a revamped section of the Adelaide market. I had already been there a few times and left again, seeing they were too busy to chat, but I could see I wouldn't ever be able to find that ideal quiet moment so I approached the counter expecting Liliana to gently brush me off. When I introduced myself and said I knew Marisa, she smiled and asked how many recipes I would like.

I was always surprised at the time people put into talking to me. Stall owners are not idle people. They work incredibly hard, and for them to spend time writing up or even just talking about what they cook at home was, to my mind, a very big ask.

These meat and eggplant
rissoles can be served hot or
at room temperature, which
means they can be made to
take on picnics. The inclusion
of the meat in this mixture
means these rissoles form the
centre piece of a main meal
and are served with salad
or vegetables along with
fresh crusty bread.

Polpettine di Carne e Melanzane

500 g eggplants

1 egg

parsley, finely chopped

freshly grated parmigiano cheese

salt and pepper to taste

500 g minced lean beef

pinch nutmeg

Peel and slice eggplants and cook in slightly salted water for about 10 minutes. Leave to cool and then squeeze to remove any excess water. Cut the slices roughly into pieces. Lightly beat the egg and add the parsley, garlic, cheese, nutmeg, salt and pepper. Mix this well with the meat and the eggplant pieces to form a paste. Shape the mixture into small balls and fry in olive oil, turning once, until they're brown.

Over the last few years there has been an explosion in the demand for fresh pastas and gnocchi. Thankfully you can now buy 'homemade' pastas and gnocchi from most good delis. There is no denying that these so-called homemade versions may be far better than the dried or frozen varieties we used only to be able to buy. Once you taste the real thing — fresh pasta or gnocchi made with your own hands — you may never be able to look at the shop-bought kind with the same degree of excitement. The difference will be as great as that between the dried version from the supermarket shelf and the fresh varieties bought from delis.

This recipe is for the gnocchi itself. You will need to have prepared a sauce of your choice to serve with these when they are cooked. I suggest a simple sauce that doesn't dominate the taste of the gnocchi.

Making fresh pasta or gnocchi is a wonderful ritual. It's true that it is a little time-consuming but the benefits (both culinary and emotional) are outstanding. The first time I made my own gnocchi I was thrilled. Obviously, it took a while to master the technique and I was covered in flour at the end, but I had great fun doing it and the taste was superb. With gnocchi it's important, not only for tradition, that you don't use a food processor at any stage. If the potatoes are over-mashed they lose their consistency and the gnocchi will fall apart in the water, so use a fork or other implement to mash the potatoes.

Gnocchi

1 kg potatoes

2$\frac{1}{4}$ cups plain flour

salt

1 egg

Boil the potatoes whole in a covered saucepan until they are completely cooked. Usually the potatoes aren't peeled, so make sure you wash them well before putting them in the pot. When cooked, drain them well and mash them while they are still warm, taking care to leave no lumps.

Turn out the mash on a clean, dry working surface. Add some of the flour to the potato and start to knead it. In a cup, beat the egg with a fork and pour it into the middle of the dough and continue to knead. Gradually add more of the flour until you have a soft but elastic dough. If the dough becomes too sticky, sprinkle it with more flour. Knead for about 10 minutes.

Cut the dough into six pieces. Take one piece of dough, sprinkle with some flour and roll it with your hands into a sausage-like shape with a diameter of about 2 cm. Slice the cylinder of dough into little squares about 3 cm long and repeat this until all the dough is cut. Then take a large fork dusted in flour. Hold it in your hand with prongs down and with your thumb squeeze the chunks of dough against the prongs, letting the gnocchi roll off onto a clean cloth. Repeat with all the chunks. They should curl up like ribbed shells as they roll off the fork.

In a large saucepan, bring water (to which you have added some salt) to the boil. Place one-third of the gnocchi in the boiling water and remove with a strainer when they rise to the top. Place in a hot serving dish and add some sauce. Keep the water boiling and repeat the operation until all the gnocchi are cooked. Add more sauce and sprinkle some parmigiano cheese on top.

These sweet ricotta balls are traditionally served, not as a dessert, but with strong espresso coffee as morning or afternoon tea. They can be had after a meal with coffee but are generally used more like a biscuit than a dessert.

Make sure the ricotta you use is bought fresh from a deli. I have seen ricotta available at supermarkets in a container, but it compares poorly to that which you buy from the dish at a deli. The fresh kind is wetter, sweeter and silkier than the dry and, I think, slightly bitter-tasting kind you buy in a plastic container.

Palline Dolci di Ricotta

500 g ricotta

2 eggs

3 tablespoons sugar

1 tablespoon flour

1 teaspoon grated lemon peel

oil for frying

Over a mixing bowl, put the ricotta through a sieve. Stir in the eggs, sugar, flour and the lemon peel. Gently stir the mixture until it combines then make the mixture into little balls about as big as a walnut. Place the balls on a clean tea-towel. Once you have used all the mixture, lightly flour the palms of your hands and slightly flatten each ball by pressing your hands gently together. Place the flattened balls back on the tea-towel and when all have been pressed, heat about a $^1/_4$ inch of oil in a pan. Gently place the balls in the oil (do this in stages so there is room in the pan to move the balls about in the oil) and fry until they are brown. Turn and brown them on the other side. When they are cooked on all sides, remove them gently from the oil and place on paper towels to absorb the excess.

When well drained, put on a serving dish. The balls can be sprinkled with castor sugar if you like them a little sweeter. One of my friends adds cinnamon to the castor sugar and it's an addition I recommend.

Franca & Mario Petrosino

Georgina's Deli, Victoria Markets

Franca and Mario own a wonderful delicatessen in Melbourne's Vic markets. If you go there, make sure to buy their semi-dried tomatoes which are the best I've ever tasted. Semi-dried tomatoes are deliciously sweet and can be used in place of sun-dried ones in most cases. I prefer the semi-dried variety to the completely dried, which I think have been a bit over-used in the last few years. Even though these delicious, sweet, soft, red rounds don't keep as well as the sun-dried variety, I don't find their perishability a problem because they never last long enough in my fridge to be preyed upon by anything other than my voracious appetite for them.

When I came back to Sydney, I searched for semi-dried tomatoes to no avail. I scoured every deli I walked past, asked friends if they had seen them anywhere and then decided they would be a treat I'd have to wait to visit Melbourne again to enjoy.

A few months later I was in a deli in Woollahra when I saw them lying centre up, red as balloons on a tray. Sprinkled with herbs and swimming in olive oil they looked beautiful.

Now I see them everywhere, yet I have to admit none have compared to the ones I got from Franca and Mario, although many come a close second.

Mario and Franca's store is on a corner in the centre of the markets and they are always happy to talk food. Theirs was our first stop whenever my son Jack and I went to the Victoria markets. Each time, no matter how many customers deep their stall was, they greeted us warmly. Leaning over the trays of pasta to rest their elbows on the glass shopfront ledge, we talked about food and they introduced me to many of the people whose recipes follow. Invariably we would leave their stall with a bag of containers filled with wonderful preserves in olive oil or chunks of parmigiano that we ate as we walked around. Their generosity was fabulous and I am eternally grateful to them for introducing me to their tomatoes, to which, I confess, I am now seriously addicted.

Baccala is salted cod that you buy in pieces from good delicatessens. The cod is heavily salted to preserve it, so it must be soaked in cold water for at least 24 hours before cooking. The water in which the fish soaks needs to be changed regularly so the salt leaves the fish and continues to dissolve into the water throughout the 24-hour period. This is another example of how Italians survived through lean months and varied their diet throughout the year by having salted, pickled or smoked produce in their larders.

Baccala with Potatoes

6 pieces of baccala

4 potatoes, peeled and chopped into large pieces

1 kg ripe tomatoes, chopped

salt and freshly ground black pepper

a handful of Italian parsley, chopped

½ cup water

In a saucepan, brown the potatoes quickly in some oil. Place the pre-soaked baccala in with the potatoes then add the tomatoes, salt, pepper, parsley and the water. Cook on very low heat until the fish pulls apart and the potatoes are tender.

To make this a single course, a *unico*, serve it with crusty wholemeal bread and salad.

Pizzaiola

eye fillet steak

fresh tomato slices, peeled

chopped and pitted Kalamata olives

Italian parsley, finely chopped

slices of fresh Italian parmigiano

Place the slices of eye fillet in an oiled frying pan. Put a slice of tomato, a few of the olive pieces, some parsley and a generous slice of the parmigiano on each piece of steak. Cover, and cook on a very low heat (because the meat is likely to be tough if it is cooked too quickly) until the meat is cooked as desired.

Serve hot with side vegetables.

You can also cook this in a slightly different but equally delicious way by placing the tomato in the pan first, topping it with sliced potato, then the piece of steak, a drizzle of olive oil, a sprinkling of both parsley and origano and finally, when the meat is cooked, adding the cheese. This variation is also cooked covered on a slow heat.

Spaghetti with Anchovies

Like Silvana Zamberlan's spaghetti with oil and garlic, Franca's recipe is very simple but tastier than most complicated pastas.

Unlike Australia where we eat pasta served as a main course, in Italy pasta is only ever served as a *primo* (first course). Italians always accompany courses with bread so the spaghetti would be presented with a fresh loaf and nothing more. The *primo* would then be followed by a main course (*secondo*) which would be served with salad and vegetables as a side dish (*contorno*).

500 g spaghetti

olive oil

2 cloves garlic, thinly sliced

anchovy fillets, chopped

parmigiano cheese, grated

freshly chopped Italian parsley

Cook spaghetti in plenty of salted and oiled boiling water.

While the spaghetti cooks, fry the garlic in olive oil until golden brown then add the chopped anchovy fillets. When the spaghetti is cooked al dente, drain it well and add it to the anchovy mixture in the pan. Heat through and mix so the sauce covers the spaghetti.

Serve sprinkled with the parmigiano cheese and chopped parsley.

Tiramisu means 'pick me up' in Italian and the reason for this dessert's name may well be in the alcohol.

You will get the best results if you make this dish when your ingredients are at room temperature, so take them out of the fridge a little time before you begin preparations.

Tiramisu

500 g mascarpone cheese

115 g sugar

4 eggs

3–4 tablespoons of rum or other spirit

400 g packet of savoiardi sponge or pavesini

strong black espresso coffee

cocoa or grated bitter chocolate

In a bowl, cream egg yolks and sugar until smooth. Separately, beat eggwhites until stiff. Gently mix in egg yolk mixture and mascarpone, a little at a time.

Mix the rum and the very strong espresso coffee in a bowl and dip the biscuits in the mixture. Lay the dipped biscuits in a serving dish. Cover biscuits with the mascarpone mixture, then layer more rum and coffee-dipped biscuits on top. Continue layering until all the mixture is used and finish with a mascarpone layer. Sprinkle with cocoa (or grated bitter chocolate). Refrigerate for at least an hour before serving.

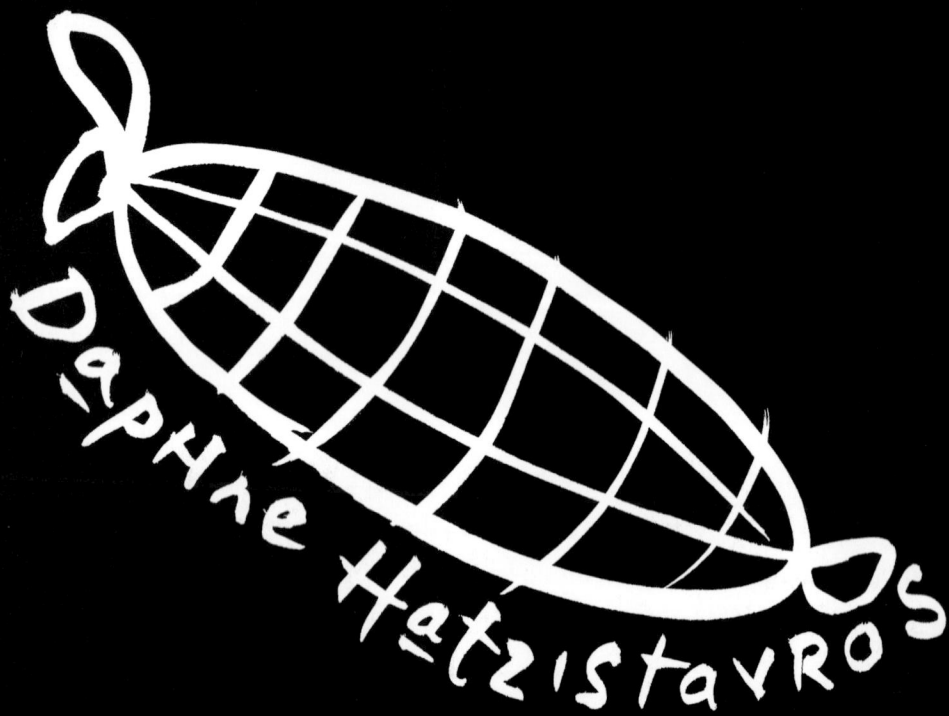

Daphne Hatzistavros

Deli Section, Victoria Markets

The dips and other homemade items for sale on Daphne's stall are true to their name — they are all made by Daphne herself. I was amazed at how she found the time and energy not only to work long hours at the stall but to then go home and cook for her family and the stall as well.

Running a market stall is not easy work. The hours are long and the days off are few and far between. On the days the markets are closed to the public, those who run stalls are usually busy restocking, ordering and, in Daphne's case, cooking. On some workers you can see the strain of many years of hard toil, but Daphne is radiant and always smiling. When I had the proof sheet made for the photos of the Vic markets, Daphne's face jumped out from the throng. Some shine, and Daphne is one of them.

While it is certainly true that some soups are best served piping hot, Daphne's soups featuring beans and lentils are intended to be eaten warm. So take the pot off the stove a few minutes before serving or let the individual bowls sit a moment before taking them to the table. Daphne serves this nourishing and hearty bean soup with anchovies or grilled herrings and black olives as a *proto piato* (first dish) or with fresh crusty bread and a Greek salad as a *yevma* (main course).

Fassolada

(Bean Soup)

$\frac{1}{2}$ kg cannellini beans

2 carrots, scraped and sliced

2 onions, finely chopped

2 fresh ripe tomatoes

1 cup olive oil

a few stalks celery, chopped

salt and pepper

Soak the beans overnight in cold water. After soaking, drain and rinse the beans thoroughly then place them in a pot. Cover the beans in water, add the vegetables and the oil and season with salt and pepper. Over a medium heat, cook the mixture for about 2 hours.

Serve while warm in individual bowls. For decoration, sprinkle a little chopped parsley over the soup and, if you like, a drizzle of Greek olive oil can be poured over each bowl for extra flavour.

It is a question of some debate,
and was the point of a recent scientific
experiment, whether or not the water
in which beans and lentils are soaked
should be discarded before cooking.
The experiment, as I understand it,
found no conclusive evidence to
suggest that the water in which beans
are soaked will cause stomach upsets.
Despite the findings of that study,
I still soak and drain beans when I
cook them and in this recipe Daphne
soaks and rinses the lentils a number
of times before finally cooking
them in fresh water.

Fakes

(Lentil Soup)

½ kg lentils

2–3 fresh ripe tomatoes, finely chopped

2 onions, finely chopped

3 cloves of garlic, crushed

¼ teacup strong vinegar

1 bay leaf

½ cup olive oil

salt and pepper

Clean the lentils and soak them in cold water overnight. After soaking, place the lentils in a large pot and bring them to the boil. Let the beans bubble for about 10 minutes, then remove from heat and drain. Return lentils to the pot and cover with fresh cold water. Add the onions, the tomatoes and the bay leaf along with the garlic and season to taste.

On a medium heat, cook for another hour and a half. About 10 minutes before removing the pot from the heat, add the vinegar and the olive oil.

Serve the soup warm with black olives or grilled herring.

Quail are very popular in Greece and are eaten all through the year. Despite their small morsels they are delicious and here, accompanied with rice and a rich sauce, they make a wonderful (*yevma*) main course.

Ortikia

(Quail in Cashew and Brandy Sauce)

6 whole quail

1 cup cashews, chopped

3 fresh ripe tomatoes, finely chopped

$\frac{1}{4}$ cup brandy

1 clove garlic, crushed

$\frac{1}{4}$ cup olive oil (for frying)

salt and pepper

1 onion, finely chopped

Cut the quail in half with a very sharp knife. Clean the inside of the birds and wash with cold running water.

In a frying pan, heat the oil and, when hot, add the quail and brown on all sides then remove from pan.

In the remaining oil, saute the onion, garlic and tomatoes for about 10 minutes. Add the quail to the mixture, spooning the sauce over them until the birds are very nearly cooked. Just before removing from the heat, add the cashews along with the brandy and the salt and pepper. Heat through so the flavours have time to be absorbed into the quail, but be careful not to overcook the birds.

Serve the quail on a bed of boiled rice with the sauce from the pan poured over the top. If your sauce has reduced and there isn't enough to serve as a gravy, after you remove the birds from the pan, turn up the heat, add a little water and stir well until your sauce is the required consistency. You could even add a splash more brandy, but be careful not to be too heavy-handed with the bottle or the alcohol will dominate the whole dish.

Traditionally, lunch is the main meal of the day in Greek households, with dinner — which is usually just a light meal more like a snack — served late in the evening. Daphne warns that this is a very rich dish and recommends it be served at lunchtime in keeping with Greek tradition, or for an early dinner so there is plenty of digestion time before going to bed.

Stifado

(Hare Ragout)

1 hare (approx. 1½ kg)

1 kg small pickling-sized onions

1 cup olive oil

1 cup vinegar

3 fresh ripe tomatoes, finely diced

2 cloves garlic, crushed

1 bay leaf

1 sprig fresh rosemary

salt

coarsely ground fresh black pepper

Cut the hare into small pieces, wash well under cold running water and drain.

Heat the oil in a pot and add the pieces of hare. Peel the onions but keep them whole and add to the pot with the hare. Saute the onions and the hare in the oil for about 10 minutes. Pour in the vinegar, add the tomatoes, the garlic, rosemary, bay leaf, salt and pepper and enough water in which to cook the hare on a low to medium heat for about 2 hours.

The idea is that the water will reduce to a thick sauce after the 2 hours, so the amount you add will vary. I suggest adding enough water to half cover the hare, but check it throughout the cooking process and add more if it looks dry.

After the 2 hours, the dish will be ready to serve with lots of crusty bread to soak up the sauce and a Greek salad with lots of feta to cut some of the richness.

Daphne told me that the last time she was in Greece she saw a big change there. Traditionally lamb has been the main meat served in Greek homes. Occasionally, she told me, a dish of baked goat would be served, but now, she says, Greeks have turned to other meats, especially beef. I'm sure that with the publicity surrounding mad cow disease there will be a sharp return to the old ways in Greece.

Lamb that is young and slaughtered during the spring months is most favoured by Grecians. The lush spring pastures give a sweetness to the meat that is absent at other times of the year.

Stuffed Leg of Lamb

1 leg of lamb (1$\frac{1}{2}$ kg)

4 slices leg ham

150 g kefalotiri cheese

1 cup white wine

1 cup butter, melted

$\frac{1}{2}$ cup chopped parsley

1$\frac{1}{2}$ kg small round potatoes

salt and pepper

Ask your butcher to remove the bone from your leg of lamb and beat the meat to spread it out, ready for rolling.

Wash the meat and lay it out flat on a clean surface. Season it with the salt and pepper then cover the meat with the parsley. Lay the slices of ham on top of the bed of parsley, then crumble the cheese over the ham. Roll up the leg of lamb and tie it with string. Gently melt the butter on the stove. Place the lamb in a heavy baking dish and then pour all the melted butter over the top.

Place in a medium to hot oven and brown the meat on all sides. When sealed, add 2 cups of water and the wine and bake for another $\frac{1}{2}$ hour.

Wash and peel the potatoes and place them in the tray whole, beside the meat. Lower the temperature of the oven to about 180°C and bake for another 1$\frac{1}{4}$ hours, adding more water if necessary. Remember that in Greece no-one eats rare meat, so all these meat dishes are cooked for some time but are still very tender when they are done.

Slice the meat in the round while it is still tied and serve it with the potatoes and a Greek salad.

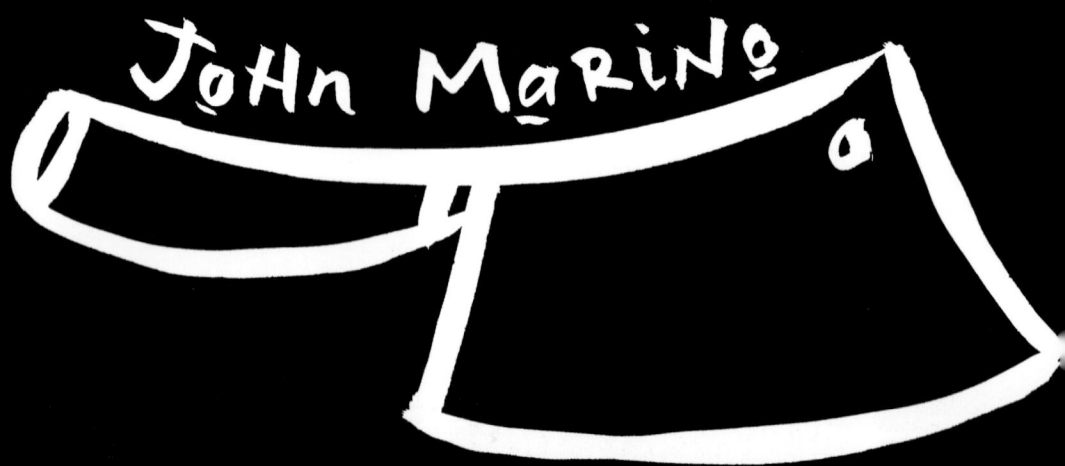

John Marino

Marino Meat & Food Store,
Central Market, Adelaide

John was recommended to me as a 'must speak to' by Lucy and Michael at Banat's stall (see page 146). Lucy said she bought all her meat from John and when I went to the shop I could see why; beautifully cured meats alongside good cuts of lean meat and an owner who loved to talk about food and some of his favourite recipes.

John's shop also sells big tins of olive oil, many pulses like chick peas and lentils as well as homemade tomato sauce in beer bottles similar to the sauce Giovanni from the Port market makes at home (see page 4).

Zampone is a boned and stuffed pig's trotter. The trotter is usually stuffed with minced pork, fennel and orange peel although the recipe will change from butcher to butcher. John wouldn't disclose his secret recipe for zampone but it is easier and better to buy it from a butcher than to make it yourself. Very few Italian families would actually ever make their own zampone. If you live in Adelaide, Marino's is the place to go for zampone. Marchetti Smallgoods in East Brunswick or NetPak in the Sydney suburb of Smithfield stock Marino's special zampone. If you can't get to Marino's or one of their distributors, many good Italian butchers will sell their own special zampone.

Zampone is traditionally served with lentils on New Year's Eve to herald in a year of prosperity. The roundness of the lentils represents coins and it is thought to be very bad luck not to include lentils in a meal on the evening before a new year.

This is a wonderful example of a dish which uses all those extra pieces of an animal we are often squeamish about eating, but which, in truth, are just too good to throw out. Sometimes I wonder whether, if we actually slaughtered our own meat, we would feel differently about the terrible waste that goes on. If a pig I had known since suckling were to be killed for my benefit, I would feel better about it if I made sure every little bit of it went to good use.

Zampone with Lentils

1 zampone

500 g lentils

80 g butter

150 g San Marino prosciutto crudo

1 onion, whole

1 carrot, whole

1 stick celery

salt and pepper to taste

Soak the zampone in cold water for 12 hours. In a separate bowl, soak the lentils for the same amount of time (or at least 3 hours). Drain the zampone.

Prick the rind of the zampone with a needle and make small incisions between the fork of the trotter to stop the skin splitting while cooking.

Immerse the zampone in cold water in a saucepan and bring to the boil. Cook on a very low heat for 3 hours.

In the meantime, bring to the boil the lentils, onion, carrot and celery. Simmer for 1½ hours in another saucepan of salted water. Drain the lentils and discard the vegetables.

Melt the butter in a saucepan, add the cubed prosciutto and simmer for 5 minutes.

Add the lentils and 50 ml of water from the zampone and cook for 10 to 15 minutes — long enough to blend the flavours. Add salt and pepper to taste and take off the stove. Drain the zampone. It will be well cooked and therefore very easy to slice. Serve the slices of zampone on top of the lentils and look forward to a prosperous new year.

Many assume that pancetta or any cured meat will be the same no matter where or from whom you buy it. Like almost anything though, some are better than others and meat is no exception. Many cured meats are too salty or too dry, but the ones you buy from Marino's are wonderfully moist and fresh. Here's a recipe that uses pancetta in a great, slightly bitter-tasting pasta sauce that is simple and very quick to make.

Pasta con Pancetta e Arugula

8 tablespoons olive oil

4 cloves garlic, crushed

200 g San Marino pancetta

1 bunch of arugula (rocket), sliced

½ bunch parsley, chopped

500 g penne

Heat oil, add garlic and pancetta. Cook until pancetta is done well, but not dry. Add greens and cook for an extra 30 seconds. Pour the green sauce over cooked penne and sprinkle with lots of parmigiano. Serve with a crusty loaf and small dishes of olive oil to dip the bread into.

Braciola is a rib-like piece of meat on the bone and this recipe is another example of creating a two-course meal from the one set of ingredients. Once cooked, the sauce from the braciola can be served on pasta as the *primo*. In this case, the braciola itself is served as a *secondo* course accompanied with side vegetables. Alternatively, because in Australia we tend to serve just one large main course, you could top the pasta with the sauce and the braciola and accompany it with salad.

As with many Italian recipes, familiarity with cooking times is important. Here, you will need to estimate when the braciola will be ready and cook the pasta so it will be perfectly al dente just as the dish is ready to serve. Co-ordinating cooking times can seem a little daunting at first, but relax and remember that dishes like this one, which have a long cooking time, are very forgiving. If you don't get the timing perfectly right, it won't matter too much. You can take the dish off the stove and let it sit with a lid on to retain the heat while the pasta cooks to perfection. Remember too that many dishes will taste better this way — not scalding hot.

Braciola alla Marino

1 kg braciola (I suggest you use pork chops for this recipe)

1 Spanish onion, chopped

2 cloves garlic, crushed

1 stick celery, chopped

$\frac{1}{2}$ cup olive oil

1 kg fresh ripe tomatoes, peeled

salt, pepper

500 g pasta of your choice

You will need a pan with a lid to make this dish successfully. Heat the oil and gently fry the onion and garlic until transparent. Add celery, salt and pepper. Cook for 2 minutes before adding braciola. Cook on a low heat with the lid on until tender (about an hour). The juices from the braciola should be enough to stop any burning or sticking, but do check it regularly to ensure it doesn't dry out. If it looks like it might catch, add a little water. When the braciola is tender, add the peeled tomatoes and cook for a further hour on medium heat with the lid off to reduce the liquid.

Just before the dish is ready to be served, cook the pasta in plenty of boiling salted water.

When the tomatoes have reduced to a thick sauce, the dish is ready and may be served as suggested above.

Nicholas Seafood Traders,
Sydney Fish Markets

Nicholas owns one of the large shops at the Sydney fish markets. Unlike many of the other markets featured in this book, the Sydney fish markets have been upgraded and the shops there are bigger and more commercial than any of the others I visited. There is a large carpark which you pay to use, a restaurant and even a cooking school. I must say, I was in two minds about whether or not to include this market in the book. In many ways I think it is a market that has lost some of its soul to commercialism, but nonetheless if you live in Sydney it is still a great place to buy fresh seafood. The commercial nature of this market meant I had some trouble getting people to contribute to this project as many of them were just too busy to take the time to talk to me. My faith was restored though when I found Nicholas who enthusiastically sat me down and talked seafood with passion and soul.

In Greece, octopus is left out in the sun to dry before it's cooked. Nicholas tells me though that the drying is not crucial to the success of this dish which uses large octopus. In Greece, different methods of cooking are used depending on the size of the octopus. Nicholas gave me methods for both large and small octopus but this one uses the bigger ones, tenderised overnight in a marinade.

BBQ Large Octopus

large octopus

garlic, crushed

fresh ripe tomatoes

olive oil

Clean the octopus. (Cut between the 'head' and beginning of the legs and remove the cartilage. Cut the 'head' open and turn it inside out to remove all the guts. Rinse under cold water.) When cleaned, cut the octopus into large chunky pieces.

Overnight, marinate the octopus in good quality olive oil, crushed garlic and chopped tomatoes. The acidity of the tomato breaks down some of the octopus fibre, making it tender.

On a very hot barbecue, cook the octopus quickly so it is seared and charred, looking almost burned.

Serve with a green salad and bread or on rice.

Someone told me that Greeks and Italians rarely use chopping boards when preparing food. This recipe explains not only how to cook small octopus, but also the method used to cut an onion in the palm of your hand.

Small Octopus

baby octopus, cleaned

garlic

olive oil

onion

fresh ripe tomatoes, chopped

red wine

Pour good quality olive oil into a pot. Add crushed garlic and an onion that you have held in your hand and chopped into cubes, first by chopping down to form a number of parallel incisions and then by cutting across at right angles, so the onion falls into small cubes. It's important not to see the onion in the dish you end up serving, so it must be cut into small cubes. Saute the onion and the garlic in the oil until golden brown.

Clean the octopus (see previous recipe), but leave it whole if it is small. Add it to the pot of garlic and onion and saute it. The octopus will lose a lot of water, so it will begin to simmer in its own juices. Add some freshly chopped tomatoes (again cubed) and simmer for about 15 minutes. The dish will turn a deep rich burgundy colour and then (and only then) pour in some red wine and simmer just a few more minutes.

If you pour the wine in too early, the acidity of it breaks down the flesh of the octopus and the dish will end up too mushy. By waiting, you get the flavour of the wine and retain the texture of the octopus.

Serve on wet rice (slightly sloppy like a risotto) with salad.

'We don't usually have three courses, there's just one, the main course,' says Nicholas as we walk around behind the counters, talking about his wonderful selection of seafood. It's quite traditional in Greek and Italian cuisine for everything to be cooked together. The parts of the meal are its whole and they are all cooked together in a wonderful blending of flavours and textures.

For a family meal, a fish would be baked in cutlets or steaks rather than in one large piece. The manner in which this dish is cooked explains why cutlets would be better than the whole fish.

Baked Fish Cutlets

6 fresh firm-fleshed fish cutlets

3–4 potatoes, peeled, depending on size

olive oil

$^3/_4$ kg fresh whole tomatoes

1 cup chopped celery

rigani

tomato paste

Put the cutlets into a baking dish with lots of good quality olive oil. Slice peeled potatoes so they will cook to tenderness in the same time as it will take to cook the fish. The thickness of the potatoes will depend on how thick the cutlets are. Nicholas says, 'Greek women have a sixth sense about how to prepare things so ingredients cook at the same time.' My suggestion is to make the potato slices about 2 cm thick. Put the slices of potato on top of the fish cutlets. Slice tomatoes and place them on top of the potatoes and add some chopped celery. Sprinkle rigani over the dish and then add a smear of tomato paste across the top. Bake in a hot oven until the fish is cooked (about 15 minutes) but check it carefully so it doesn't overcook.

When you pick up a cutlet, it will have the potato and tomato on top and each cutlet therefore makes an individual meal.

Serve with salad and crusty bread.

'Back home we don't make a separate stock when we make soups. The flavour of the stock is generated by what we put in the soup and eat,' says Nicholas. This recipe is one Nicholas's mother often made for him and he has a nostalgic look in his eyes when he describes it to me.

This is a very sweet-tasting soup and Nicholas could never understand why his mother used an onion studded with whole cloves to make the stock. 'It was only recently, when I was talking to a French chef who buys from me, that I realised why my mother used the cloves. I asked the chef how she made fish soup that wasn't really "fishy". She said her secret was to include a tiny pinch of curry powder in the water. Suddenly it all made sense to me. My mother must have known that something in the spice makes this a really sweet, not too fishy-smelling soup. It's absolutely beautiful,' he said excitedly.

Traditional Fish Soup

whole fresh firm-fleshed fish
like snapper or bream

olive oil

1 cup celery, chopped

a whole onion

3 whole cloves

$^3/_4$ kg fresh whole ripe tomatoes,
peeled and chopped

2 potatoes, peeled and cubed

1 tablespoon tomato paste

1 cup of rice

Gut and carefully scale the fish. Even if a shop scales my fish, I always go over it again with a very sharp knife, paying particular attention to the areas around the tail and head, to make sure all the scales are removed. There's nothing worse than biting into delicate fish and getting a mouthful of scales. Cut the fish up into four big pieces.

Immerse the fish in cold salted water and pour in some olive oil. Add the chopped celery and potatoes (cube the potatoes quite small so they cook through in the time it takes to make the stock). Stud the onion with the cloves and add it whole, along with the peeled tomatoes, to the water and fish.

Bring the fish to the boil and simmer for 20 minutes. The soup should have a fish flavour to it but if you cook the soup for too long it will have a bitter taste. Carefully lift the fish out of the water and put aside. Take the cloves out of the onion and discard them. Pour the stock with the onion, the potato and the tomatoes still in it through a thick sieve. With a wooden spoon or a mouli grind the vegetables through the sieve. This will thicken the soup and also ensure no loose bones or scales get into the broth.

Stir in a tablespoon or more of tomato paste to taste. Add about a cup of rice to the broth, take it back to the stove and cook until the rice is tender. Don't use too much rice, remembering it multiplies by three times. The rice is not a feature of this dish, it's merely there to add carbohydrate as nourishment and act as a thickener for the broth.

While the rice is cooking take all the fish off the bone and when the rice is done, drop the fish gently back into the soup. Simmer for a minute or two just to heat through and serve with crusty bread.

According to Nicholas, this sardine dish is not one to 'cook when you've got the boss coming over for dinner. You've got to get into the fish with your hands and it's pretty messy.'

Grilled Sardines with Rich Sauce

large sardines, whole

olive oil

garlic

fresh ripe tomatoes, diced

rigani

tomato paste

Clean good-sized sardines by pulling the heads off towards the tail, so the guts come out all in one go with the head. Rinse them in cold water and rub them in olive oil.

Fry garlic in olive oil and add diced ripe tomatoes and rigani. This should be a very thick and oily sauce so use lots of oil. Simmer for about 10 minutes and if the sauce doesn't thicken up enough, add some tomato paste.

Grill or barbecue the sardines quickly on a very hot oiled grill or plate. Once cooked, put the sardines on a serving platter and pour over the rich oil sauce. Let it sit for a moment (but not so long that it goes cold) to allow the flavours to mingle before serving.

Serve with salad and bread.

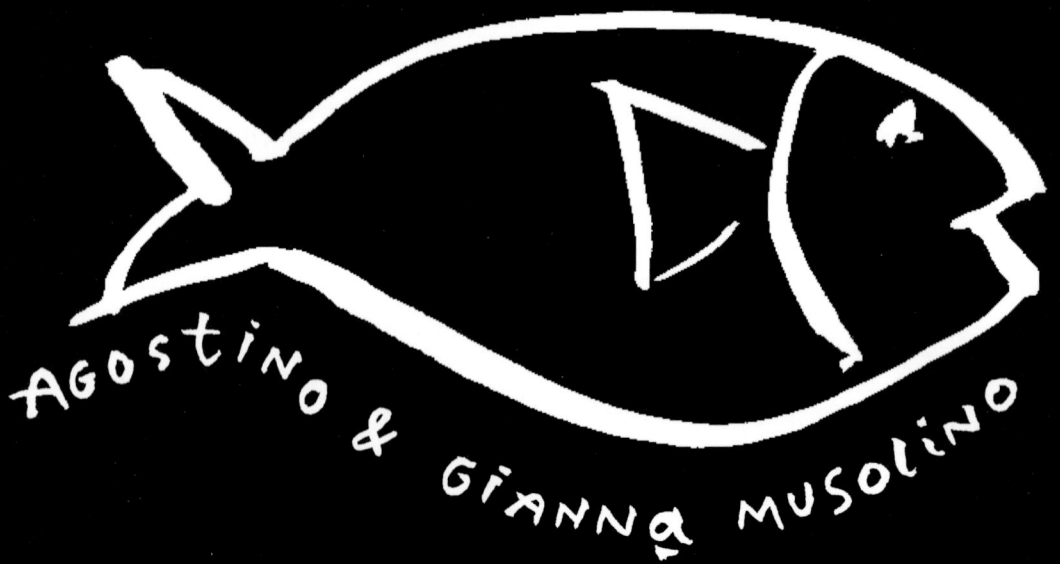

Agostino & Gianna Musolino

Cyril's Superior Fruit and Veg,
Central Market, Adelaide

Cyril's is perhaps the most famous fruit and veg stall at the Adelaide markets. Agostino (Gus) and his brother Rocky are always there, along with other members of the Musolino family who aren't constant fixtures but appear regularly to help out with the family business. There is always a great deal of noise emanating from the stall. People are encouraged to taste the fruit, so there's usually a bowl of fresh ripe whatever's-in-season resting on a pile of rock-melons or potatoes at the front of the stall.

The boys all wear bright pink T-shirts, and each time I visited the stall Rocky would be wearing a sticking plaster exactly the same shade of pink across the side of his face. Gus would tell me it was because he'd just been in a fight but no other part of him ever looked battered and I'm sure it was there more for a laugh than anything else. A very funny sight too — big Rocky in his pink T-shirt and fluorescent band-aid to match, selling superb fruit and vegetables.

The afternoon a journalist from the *Adelaide Advertiser* found out about this book she dragged me kicking and screaming down to the markets for a photo opportunity. I hate having my photo taken at the best of times, but I thought this little expedition would shoot any credibility I had at the market. I was in my very best suit with a lather of make-up on my face looking, I thought, like an idiot. Well, I was right to worry. Gus and his brothers thought it was a hoot. I'd been at the markets at six o'clock that morning and needless to say I hadn't been wearing my suit then.

'What's the big occasion, Caro?' they yelled out between sniggers from the stall. 'She doesn't normally look like that,' they hollered to the journalist.

'Ha, ha, I'll get you guys. You'll keep,' I retorted, then thought of the perfect way. I winked at Rocky, who hadn't been one of the loud ones, and turned to the journalist. 'How about we get the guys from Cyril's in the shot?'

She thought it was a great idea, so there we all stood, feeling stupid as we held bundles of fruit and vegetables up to the camera.

When I first talked to Agostino about this book, he told me he wasn't big on cooking. There seems to have been a shift in Italian families between men like Agostino, who have grown up in Australia, and their fathers. As this book shows, many of the men of the older generation are keen cooks. They may not partake in the day-to-day preparation of the family meals; however, they do have their own specialities. Particularly, the men are involved with things like salami-making and the curing of meats but they seem also to have an understanding of food and how to cook.

Agostino told me that his wife did most of the cooking and explained that their tastes and methods had been greatly influenced by Australian culture. Agostino was quick to mention, though, that his Mum, Gianna, was a great traditional cook and offered to ask her to contribute some of her specialities. Unlike many other people in this book whose recipes feature ingredients they sell on their stalls, these from the Musolino family were chosen because they were Agostino's favourites.

Dishes like crocchette di pesce, that make use of fish or meat in small quantities, were traditionally prepared as a way of making a little protein go a long way. Obviously, when there was an abundance of fresh meat or fish, dishes like this would stand aside in favour of meals featuring whole fillets or slices of meat.

Crocchette
di Pesce

500 g shredded fish fillets (fish of your choice)

½ litre milk (more or less)

50 g butter

60 g plain flour

100 g grated parmigiano

salt and pepper to taste

a pinch of nutmeg

For frying you will need:

1 egg

1 tablespoon of plain flour

breadcrumbs

oil

Melt butter in a saucepan. Add flour and pour in milk slowly, stirring until you have a smooth mixture that is quite dense. Essentially you are making a bechamel at this stage. While the mixture is still warm, add the parmigiano and mix well, add the shredded fish and remaining ingredients and continue mixing until all the ingredients have combined. With this mixture you will then make crocchette by rolling portions of the mixture into balls (about the size of large meat balls) with your hands. If the mixture sticks to your hands, rub a little flour onto your palms.

As you make each crocchetta, roll it in flour, then in beaten egg, then in breadcrumbs. Fry the crocchetta in hot oil. When they are brown and cooked through, place each crocchetta on a paper towel to absorb excess oil. Once drained, place on a serving platter or individual plates and serve with salad and fresh crusty bread.

As the name suggests, crostata is really just an open tart that has criss-crosses of pastry as its top. Crostata can be filled with any ingredients of your choice but is usually made *di marmellata* (with jam) as this recipe describes.

However, a more elaborate recipe has as its filling a wonderful mixture of fresh ricotta, lemon rind, 3 egg yolks, $\frac{1}{3}$ cup of sugar, 2 tablespoons of plain flour and a pinch of cinnamon or nutmeg. If you like the idea of this mixture, simply follow the recipe opposite for making pastry for the base and top and substitute all the ingredients above, gently mixed together in a bowl, for the jam.

Connie Rotolo gave me a recipe for Pastiera Napoletana, a delicious variation on this recipe which includes ricotta and arborio rice. It appears later in the book (page 207).

C r o s t a t a

1 heaped teaspoon of cream of tartar

1 level tablespoon of bicarbonate soda

250 g butter

400 g sugar

rind of one lemon, grated

4 eggs

jam (usually red jam is used in this
crostata — i.e. strawberry, plum or cherry)

Melt butter in a saucepan. Beat eggs by hand then add the rest of
the ingredients together with the butter. On a clean dry surface, lightly
dusted with plain flour, knead the mixture until you have a smooth, stiff
pastry. Roll out the dough and put aside enough pastry to make about
8 long, thin strips which you will use to make the criss-cross lid of
the pie.

Line a round, buttered baking tin (about the size of a cheesecake tray
with sides at least 3–4 cm high) with the remainder of the pastry. Fill with
red jam of your choice (or the ricotta mixture as described above) and
carefully lay the pastry strips across the tart in a criss-cross manner.

Bake in a pre-heated 150°C oven until golden in colour and crisp all
over. This will usually take about an hour.

Edina

Port Adelaide Market

The market at Port Adelaide is very ad hoc. Out in the open air, people sell from the back of their trucks or cars, from trestle tables they erect and pile high with produce, or simply out of boxes.

Edina sells from two card tables if I remember correctly and while she doesn't ever have huge quantities of produce, it is always of a wonderful quality. The vegetables she sells are grown in her own garden. She often has long ropes of garlic heaped in a pile on her tables, beside which sit fresh sweet seasonal vegetables. Edina shades herself and her produce under a large umbrella, so she's easily recognisable.

This dish makes use of myriad spring vegetables which combine to make a sweet meal. The recipe here includes veal, but Edina says this is a dish that works equally well without the meat.

You do not need to use the vegetables suggested in the recipe — this is a versatile dish where you can add whatever spring vegetables you have on hand. Fresh young broad beans, chopped zucchini, tender chopped young artichokes all work well.

Peas with Spring Vegetables

500 g freshly shelled peas

bunch of asparagus, cut into pieces

250 g veal or steak, diced

$\frac{1}{2}$ medium onion, finely chopped

1 medium potato, diced

garlic cloves to taste

1 tablespoon olive oil

nut of butter

handful of chopped Italian parsley

a splash of wine (red or white)

salt and pepper to taste

Pour oil into saucepan, add onion, garlic, meat and parsley and saute them gently. When meat has browned, pour in the wine and stir until the wine reduces (approximately 8–10 minutes). Add potatoes, peas and asparagus. Cook for a few minutes before adding the butter, salt and pepper. Don't forget to keep stirring! Cook a little longer. Add approximately 2 cups of water. Bring back to the boil. Simmer with lid agape for approximately 10 minutes.

Serve with fresh crusty bread.

Stella

D&J Poultry, Prahran Markets, Melbourne

The Prahran market is divided into sections. There's the main part where all the fruit and vegetable stalls are situated along with a fabulous flower shop where you can buy huge bunches of flowers or small trees in pots to take home and plant. At the front of the market, near the main street, all the delis line up displaying their wonderful wares in big glass jars or huge terracotta pots. Here, in this section, is a bread shop where loaves of most descriptions can be bought freshly baked.

In another section of the market you will find meat and fresh seafood shops. I must say I think the meat in the Melbourne markets is some of the best I've ever seen. At Prahran and also at the Vic markets, the meat is incredibly lean and always very fresh looking. I was really quite surprised by the quality which stands head and shoulders above anything I've seen in Sydney, except perhaps for meat from Asian butcheries, which also display their meat well trimmed and fresh.

Here, alongside the meat and seafood, you will find Stella and her shop specialising in fresh poultry and game birds.

The following recipe for quail can be cooked on a barbecue, on top of the stove in a frying pan, or baked in the oven. Whichever way, it's quick to cook and the marinade is simple to prepare for a delicate meal.

Marinated Quail

6 quail

$\frac{1}{2}$ cup olive oil

garlic, crushed

rigani

salt and pepper

freshly squeezed lemon juice
(to taste, but about $\frac{1}{2}$ a cup)

Cut the quail down the centre to make a butterfly. Place in a large bowl.
Mix together all of the remaining ingredients then pour over the quail.
Stir to coat, then cover the bowl and refrigerate overnight.

If you barbecue the quail, cook them for about 5 minutes each side.

If frying, they take about 7 minutes each side and if baking they will
be cooked in 30 minutes in a moderate oven. Whichever method you
choose, baste them in the marinade while cooking.

Serve on a bed of rice with a Greek salad.

Stella's contribution to this book needs special thanks. She wrote these recipes at a time when her daughter was in hospital and I'm especially grateful to her for sending them.

When I first got this recipe I thought, my god, where am I going to find vine leaves. I mentally perused the shelves of the local deli and every other shop I could think of before kicking myself at my stupidity. I rang a friend whose back yard I had spent many afternoons sitting in, under the shade of a wonderful grape vine, and asked if I could come and visit.

I returned home with the casing for these rolls. If you have no vine, then carefully peel off the large outer leaves of a whole cabbage.

Since making Stella's rolls I have seen vine leaves for sale in delis. Some sell them in tins, while others have them stacked on top of each other, already parboiled, on plates in their fridges.

Stella's Vine or Cabbage Rolls

1 kg minced chicken

pepper

salt

cinnamon

2 tablespoons fresh mint, finely chopped

$\frac{1}{2}$ cup fresh parsley, finely chopped

3 medium onions, finely chopped

6 fresh tomatoes, chopped roughly

1$\frac{1}{2}$ cups white rice

juice of 2 lemons

vine or cabbage leaves

5 tablespoons of oil

In a bowl, place all the ingredients except the oil, lemon juice and the leaves.

Mix gently until well combined then set aside. Rinse the cabbage or vine leaves well in hot water to remove any grit.

Place the leaves in a pot of boiling water and cook for 3 minutes until softened so they won't break when rolled. Remove from the pot, shake off any extra water and put on a plate.

On another plate or clean workbench, place one leaf and spoon some of the chicken mixture into the centre in a long cylindrical shape. First tuck each end in over the mixture then gently roll the leaf around the filling. Remember that the rice will expand when cooked, so don't roll too tightly or fill the leaf too full. Repeat this method until all the mixture is used. Keep a few extra leaves to line the pot.

When all the leaves have been rolled, pour the oil into a pot and turn so it covers the bottom evenly. Line the bottom of the pot with leaves then carefully place the rolls on top, following the shape of the pot around and around. When all the rolls are in the pot lying in a circular pattern, place a few leaves on top of the rolls, then pour in 3 cups of water and the juice of the lemons.

Place a flat plate on top of the leaves and then, on the plate, place another saucepan half filled with water to weigh the rolls down so they don't float and break up. Put a lid on the pot and cook for about 45 minutes on a very low heat.

When the cooking time is up, turn the heat off and leave the pot to sit for 15 minutes before opening. Remove the saucepan, the plate and the extra leaves and serve the rolls with lemon wedges, crusty bread and salad.

Giuseppina & tina Fazzolari

flour

Port Adelaide Markets

Over the last 6 months I have been holding dinner parties to test the wonderful treats I've discovered at the markets. One in particular was not like any other dinner party I'd held before. It was the night I decided to test Giuseppina's recipe for homemade spaghetti. When guests arrived I was covered in white dust and the kitchen floor looked like a snow storm had just swept through the neighbourhood. I greeted each one of them with a hand as sticky as children's clag from wet spaghetti dough. Hardly an elegant beginning to a feast, but a feast it was and the greatest success was Giuseppina's spaghetti.

I had been told that eating freshly made homemade spaghetti was like trying a completely different dish to any made with commercial pasta, but I must admit I never could quite believe it until that day when I covered myself in flour and eggs, armed myself with a rolling pin and made it myself.

Even though my first attempt was a little rough and some of the strands a little thick, I was sold — this really is something to try. I made the sauce with the words of Emilio Vairo (whose story appears on page 21) ringing in my ears. As I went to the fridge to find that extra something to add to the sauce, I remembered him saying to me as we walked around his back yard inspecting his vegetable patch, 'You not put too much in Caro, or you lose the flavours.' He was right, of course, but on this occasion I was not only interested in retaining the flavours but highlighting my efforts with the rolling pin as well!

Giuseppina and her husband run a stall selling fruit and vegetables at the Port Adelaide markets, and beside them their daughter Tina runs another. Giuseppina is a small woman who has spent so many of her years bent over in work that she is permanently stooped. She speaks little English, so Tina helped with these recipes.

For Christmas presents last year, I used a dozen eggs and a lot of flour, and made my friends Giuseppina's spaghetti which I wrapped in beautiful tea-towels and tied with raffia.

None of the Italians I spoke to had any idea of the measurements used to make pasta. Once you have made it a few times, you will understand how many eggs will absorb into the flour. When you ask an Italian how many grams of flour they use when they make spaghetti they will probably look at you as if you just asked them if the Pope is Catholic. I asked a number of people about measurements and none could give me an answer. 'As much as you need … ,' 'You know, it depends how big the eggs are,' 'I don't know, we just make it so it feels right,' were just some of the replies I got. I had to consult Marcella Hazan for measurements but suggest you do use your intuition after you've made it once. A safe bet is that you will need about 100 g of flour per egg and the following measurements will make enough spaghetti for six people, remembering that in Italy spaghetti is only ever a *primo* dish. Making spaghetti is definitely something to do with feeling, so experiment and enjoy.

Giuseppina's Homemade Spaghetti

300 g unbleached plain flour

3 eggs

On a clean dry bench, make a mound of flour with a well in the centre. If you wear jewellery, I suggest you remove it, because this gets very messy and sticky before it turns into beautiful spaghetti. In a cup, beat the eggs, then tip them into the centre of the flour. Mix the egg into the flour until it is combined. It will be very sticky at this stage, but knead the dough and sprinkle flour on the bench as you knead. If the dough continues to stick to your hands, it is too moist, so sprinkle more flour on until it is moist but not sticky. Be careful not to make the dough too dry by adding too much flour — do it slowly and knead for a few moments before adding more flour each time. Continue kneading for at least 10 minutes until the dough is smooth, moist and malleable. Your hands shouldn't have any more dough stuck to them, but if they do, wash them under cold water and dry them thoroughly before returning to the dough.

Wash the bench to remove any clumps of dough that may have stuck to the surface. Dry the bench thoroughly before sprinkling it with a light dusting of flour. Pour some olive oil into the palm of your hand and rub it into the rolling pin. Begin to roll out the dough in a circle. If the dough sticks to the bench, gently lift it and lightly flour the bench again.

Continue rolling the dough out into a large circle. It should take about 10–15 minutes to get the paper-thin disk you need. Move the dough around as you roll so it remains in a disk shape and remember, the thinner the better. If you have one section of the disk thicker than another, it will make the pasta different thicknesses and make cooking evenly a problem.

When the dough is paper thin, drape one half of the circle over the end of the bench so it hangs down. This will stretch it out a bit more, but also dry the dough out so it doesn't stick together when cutting. Leave it hanging for about 15 minutes depending on how hot the day is. If it's a dry windy day, you may only need to hang it for 10 minutes. Use your judgment — the dough needs to be moist but not wet, yet not dry enough to be brittle.

When that side is finished, rotate the disk so the other half hangs over the bench and leave as before.

When both sides have been draped over the bench it is time to cut the disk into pasta for cooking. Gently roll the dough up into a long cylinder. Take care not to roll too tightly or it will stick together and the strands of spaghetti won't separate.

With a very sharp knife, slice the cylinder the same way you cut folded crepe paper to make long streamers. Each coin-like shape you make will become a strand of spaghetti so take care to cut it very finely. After each cut, grab an end, shake out the strand and put it on the bench. Continue cutting and shaking out each strand until the roll is completely used.

Put the separated strands loosely in a bowl and cover it with a clean tea-towel. When you are ready to cook your spaghetti, boil lots of lightly salted water and drop the spaghetti loosely into the pot. Fresh pasta doesn't take as long to cook as dried, but you will need to test it as you go because cooking time will depend upon the thickness of your strips.

Pour yourself a nice glass of wine and enjoy the fruits of your labour — be sure everyone else will.

Giuseppina often sells large bags of eggplants which she holds out in her strong hands to tempt passing shoppers. In fact it was thanks to one of Giuseppina's bags that this book was born. My father loves the Port Adelaide markets and it was he who first took me there early one Sunday morning and introduced me to all the stall owners he buys from.

I had just been in Melbourne and in my spare time had been to the Vic markets with the excuse of buying some basil, but I really just wanted to wander through the aisles, absorb the noise and the exotic smells and feel the vibrance of the big sell. I had my camera with me and took a series of black and white shots of the people behind the stalls. When my stepmother Becky told me she'd been to the Port Adelaide markets and bought a huge bag of eggplants from Giuseppina and asked her how she cooked them, the idea for this book was born. Becky went straight home and followed the instructions given to her by Giuseppina, used all the eggplants, and said the results were delicious.

So, as you can see, from strange and seemingly unconnected events are books born. Here47 is the recipe that Giuseppina gave Becky which led to this book.

Giuseppina's Traditional Italian Spaghetti Sauce

12 large ripe tomatoes

1 onion, diced

1 large eggplant

$\frac{1}{2}$ cup fresh breadcrumbs (fine)

$\frac{1}{2}$ cup grated parmigiano cheese

fresh basil leaves, shredded

olive oil

pinch salt

In a blender, chop the tomatoes until they are almost liquid and put aside. In a saucepan, fry the onions in olive oil until they are golden brown. Add the tomato pulp, salt and shredded basil leaves to taste. Simmer on a low heat for about 15–20 minutes, until sauce has reduced.

Cut the peeled eggplant into strips and fry in about 4 tablespoons of olive oil until soft and brown. Remove from heat and drain off excess oil. Add the eggplant to the tomato mixture then add the cheese and the breadcrumbs and stir to combine.

Remove from heat or the cheese will stick to the pan, but keep warm while the sauce is cooking. Alternatively, put the pasta on to cook so it is ready just before you add the cheese and the breadcrumbs so they are ready to serve at the same time.

Cook spaghetti in lots of boiling salted water till al dente, drain well and serve in individual bowls. Top with sauce and serve with crusty bread.

The following pizza is not the kind we usually see in pizza shops. If anything it is more like a Turkish pizza in that the tomato topping is covered in dough, like a pasty. This pocket-like 'calzone' is a nice change to the bubbling mozzarella kind.

Traditional Pizza

small piece of fresh yeast (about the size of a 20 cent coin)

2 cups plain flour

1 cup warm water

salt

1 cup black olives, seeded and chopped

few ripe tomatoes

origano

2 cloves garlic, crushed

3 tablespoons olive oil

1 small jar anchovies

Dissolve the yeast in a bowl with the warm water. Add 2 or 3 pinches of salt and stir to ensure well dissolved. Add the flour and mix to make a medium to firm dough. You may need to add a little more warm water if the dough is too dry. Knead well until the dough is smooth and well combined. Put the dough back in a clean dry bowl and cover with a tea-towel until it doubles in size.

Peel the tomatoes by immersing them in boiling water until the skin cracks, then chop and place in a separate bowl. Add a pinch of salt, the olive oil, a pinch of origano and the garlic and stir to combine.

When the dough has doubled in size, grease a small pizza tray (about 20 cm) with olive oil. Pour a little oil into the palms of your hands and divide the dough into two equal parts, then spread one portion of the dough out over the tray, using your fingers to push it to the edges. Spread the tomato mixture over the dough, sprinkle with the olives then lay the anchovy pieces over the top. Spread the remaining dough out over the top of the tray, gently stretching it so it covers the bottom layer of pizza completely.

Bake in a moderate to hot oven until golden brown.

Lucy & Michael

Banat's Fine Foods,
Stall 38, Central Market, Adelaide

Lucy and Michael are a great team. I had a zoom lens with me at the markets and I spent a lot of time just wandering around, taking shots and getting to know people. Every time I saw Lucy and Michael they seemed to be laughing and I think they thought I was joking when I told them about this book. Lucy laughed her head off and said, 'Nah, I don't do anything special.' I looked around the stall, worried as she started to talk about how busy she was; I could see she was about to steal away! Somehow there's always a pivotal moment and I could see that if I didn't do or say something very quickly, she would make up her mind that either she had nothing worth giving me or else was too busy. I scanned the shop and saw a wonderful jar of young artichokes in deep rich green olive oil.

'Who did those?' I asked.

'Oh, we do,' she said as though it were nothing special at all.

As was so often the case in the course of researching this book, a little prompting brought out great gems.

Lucy and Michael have their own artichoke farm, so the ones that you buy from their stall have been planted, picked and finally preserved by their own hands. This recipe ensures you have artichokes on hand throughout the year to use in sauces, with salads or as part of an antipasto. Most preserved artichokes you buy from the supermarket are preserved in cheap oil, and this I believe spoils the taste. Make your own preserved artichokes by using good quality olive oil and taste the difference.

Marinated Artichokes

fresh artichokes

vinegar

garlic

bay leaves

parsley

chilli

salt and pepper

extra virgin olive oil

a large sterilised jar or jars

Remove the hard outer leaves and chop off the tough top ends of the artichokes. Immerse them in cold water to remove any dirt. Chop each artichoke into quarters or eighths if they are especially large or to suit the size of your jar. As you chop, put them into a bowl of water that has a dash of vinegar in it. This will stop the artichokes going black while you work.

Put the artichokes in boiling water with a dash of vinegar and a sprinkle of salt. Boil the artichokes until they are tender then drain them in a colander. When cool, squeeze out as much water as you can from each one. Pack the artichokes tightly into a sterilised jar with garlic, bay leaves, parsley and chilli, if you like zing! Disperse the seasonings evenly through the jar so the flavours impregnate all the artichokes. When the jar is packed, pour in good quality olive oil until the artichokes are covered and seal.

Be sure to only use clean implements when taking the artichokes out of the jar. If you put dirty utensils into the jar, they can spoil the artichokes and make them ferment.

Usually in Australia, we serve artichokes in the French way — boiled until tender and accompanied with a lemon and butter sauce into which you dip each individual leaf and then the tender heart. That is a delicate and extremely good way to serve artichokes but sometimes you will want something a little more substantial. Here's a recipe for stuffed artichokes that looks great when served on platters. The stuffing between the leaves spills out and reminds me of a Christmas pinecone crammed full of surprises.

Stuffed Artichokes

fresh whole artichokes

2 eggs, beaten

$^3/_4$ cup parmigiano cheese, grated

$^1/_2$ cup pecorino cheese, grated

a handful of breadcrumbs (fresh, not from a box)

finely chopped fresh parsley

salt and pepper

Prepare the artichokes as directed in the previous recipe, but do not cut them into pieces. Be sure to immerse them in the vinegared water as directed to stop them going black. In a bowl, combine the eggs, the grated cheeses, breadcrumbs, parsley and salt and pepper.

Remove the artichokes from the vinegared water and squeeze them dry. Cut the stem to about 3 cm from the artichoke itself. It will need to sit on its stem, but it should be short.* Gently open out the leaves, taking care not to break them off from the heart and pack the stuffing tightly in between them. Open up the middle as much as possible without breaking it and pack as much stuffing as you can into the cavity.

Sit the artichokes on their stems in a baking dish of water about 1 cm deep that has a large dash of oil and some salt in it. Bake in a medium oven until tender. This will usually take about 45 minutes but the cooking time will depend on the size and maturity of the artichokes. A good test is to pull one of the centre leaves off the artichoke. If it comes away easily, it is cooked. If it's hard to remove, then return it to the oven.

* The leftover stems can be used as part of the stuffing if peeled and chopped finely.

Lucy's Almond Bread

These thin slices of almond bread are served with coffee after dinner or for morning or afternoon tea. Traditionally, these dry biscuits are not served as a dessert but are dipped into liquid. A friend remembers, as a child, dipping almond bread into vin santo — a fortified wine similar to muscat or marsala. In Italy small amounts of alcohol are not seen as harmful to children and they are often encouraged to sip wine at the dinner table. My friend also says she dipped these treats into a zabaglione mixture, which is full of wonderful sweet muscat. I loved these biscuits dipped into Connie Rotolo's rich creamy panna cotta (see page 193). There is a lot of sugar in these biscuits and if you think they will be too sweet, reduce the amount you use.

1 dozen eggwhites

4 cups plain flour

4 cups castor sugar

3 cups almond slivers

pinch of salt

1/2 teaspoon vanilla sugar

With clean dry beaters, beat the eggwhites with a pinch of salt until they are thick and stiff. Add the vanilla sugar and the castor sugar and beat for about 3 minutes. Add the flour and beat until well mixed. Gently fold in the almonds.

Mould into a bread-like shape and bake on a baking dish in a moderate oven until crisp and a light golden colour. Remove from the oven and when cool cut into thin slices and bake again until crisp.

Frank Schirripa

Central Market Mushroom, Stall 68,
Central Market, Adelaide

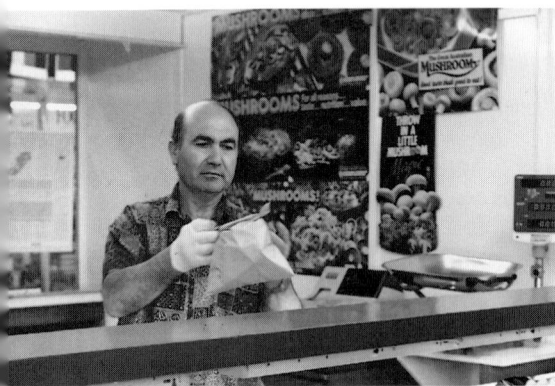

Frank's stall at the Central Market has been selling the most superb mushrooms for as long as I can remember. When I worked at the markets I would always stop off on my way home to buy a bag of mushies from stall number 68. There was no point ever looking around for mushrooms — theirs were the best and I was a loyal customer. It has always been a stall specialising only in mushrooms and recently the range has been extended to include exotic varieties. You can choose from small tight buttons and huge open field mushrooms, and now the 'wild' but cultivated mushrooms we have added to the Australian cuisine can be found there as well. To my memory, not much else has changed at this stall where boxes and boxes of unblemished fungi sit along the counter, almost too perfect to be real.

Marinated Mushrooms

When preserving mushrooms, the tight buttons are used because they keep their shape and don't break when packed tightly into a jar. These marinated mushrooms, sweet and full of flavour, look great added to an antipasto.

champignon mushrooms (enough to pack tightly into the jar of your choice)

fresh garlic, crushed

fresh chillis, chopped (optional)

a mixture of fresh origano and parsley, finely chopped

salt and pepper

good quality olive oil

Bring a pot of salted water to the boil. Plunge the mushrooms into the pot for about 4 or 5 minutes. The mushrooms should be tender but not soft so the cooking time will depend on their size. When tender, drain and then plunge the mushrooms into cold water to stop any further cooking. Drain by shaking the colander to remove excess water from the mushrooms.

Pack the mushrooms into a sterilised jar with the garlic and herbs, and the chopped chilli if you like a spicy mix, making sure to disperse them evenly through the mushrooms. Grind in lots of black pepper and some sea salt then top up the jar with good quality olive oil. Seal tightly.

When removing mushrooms from the jar be sure to use clean utensils, otherwise the remaining mushrooms will go mouldy. The mushrooms must be submerged in the olive oil, so top it up each time it gets low.

Stuffed
Mushrooms

large button or any mushrooms big enough to hold stuffing

½ kg pork and veal mince

1 egg, beaten

1 cup fresh breadcrumbs

1 cup parmigiano, grated

freshly chopped parsley

ground pepper and salt to taste

Cut the stems off the mushrooms, leaving the caps whole. Dice the stems and in a bowl mix them together with the other ingredients.

Gently fry the mixture in olive oil just until the meat cooks through, then set aside.

Plunge mushroom caps into boiling, lightly salted water until tender but not soft. When tender, drain before quickly plunging into cold water to stop further cooking. Once cooled, drain again and gently squeeze out as much water as you can from the cooked mushrooms, taking care not to break them.

Pack the individual mushroom caps with plenty of the stuffing mixture. Gently fry the stuffed mushrooms in olive oil until dark in colour and cooked through, or bake in a tray with olive oil in a moderate oven.

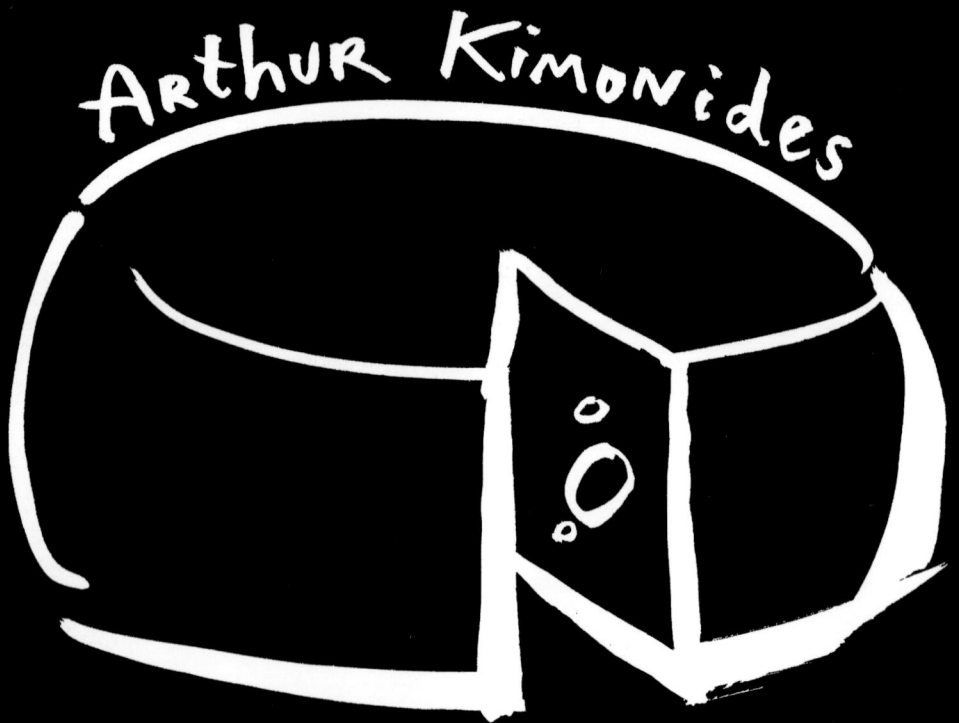

Arthur Kimonides

Kimo's Deli, Prahran Markets, Melbourne

Arthur's shop in the Prahran markets is full of continental delicacies — cured meats, fresh cheeses and a wide variety of Greek cheeses often quite hard to find in some places.

Since I've been writing this book, my son has developed quite a passion for octopus. Whenever we go to the fish markets he begs me to buy and cook them for him. The shop assistants at Arthur's deli were a little shocked to be serving marinated octopus to a seven-year-old. They looked at me with an expression that said, 'Are you sure this is okay? I don't really think he's going to like it.' I nodded and explained his passion for these tentacled creatures from the sea. Out of all the goods at Arthur's deli, I wasn't in the least surprised to hear him asking for the 'oci'. He ordered a big tub, which we ate as we walked around the markets. It was very good, so we did a lap of the stalls then made our way back to Arthur's to ask if he'd include the octopus we'd just eaten in the selection of recipes he was getting together for the book. He kindly agreed and here it is.

The octopus in the following recipe reduces in bulk quite considerably. Here, for example, the 10 kilograms of octopus reduces to about 2 $\frac{1}{2}$ kilograms. Still, this is probably more than you'd use for one sitting, so you might like to halve the ingredients. Or the octopus will keep quite well if stored in a clean airtight container in the fridge. This is the perfect dish to be served as part of any *mezethes* and it's especially good with black olives and crusty bread. Even though the marinade is quite acidic, I like this served with fresh lemon wedges for squeezing.

Arthur's Marinated Octopus

10 kg large octopus

8–10 cloves

freshly crushed garlic

2 grated onions

rigani

¼ cup virgin olive oil

½ cup lemon juice

½ cup vinegar

Gut and clean the octopus and remove the skin. Wash thoroughly under cold running water, taking care to remove any sand from the suckers.

Put the octopus in a large pot. Don't add any water or liquids, but put the octopus on a high heat on the stove and cook for about 5 minutes. The idea is to remove the moisture from the flesh. Strain off the water, then repeat the process to further remove water. Strain again, then cook until octopus turns a purple or red colour.

Remove the octopus from the pot and discard any liquid. Let the octopus cool before cutting into bite-sized pieces. Put the pieces into a large bowl and add the garlic and onion. Stir in the rigani and the olive oil. Add salt to taste and then pour in the vinegar and lemon juice. Mix well to combine and leave at room temperature to cool for at least an hour before putting it in the refrigerator.

The following fried cheese pieces are perfect as part of a *mezethes* with black olives and crusty bread. Arthur told me that at home haloumi cheese is served for breakfast with eggs. I couldn't quite imagine the combination first thing in the morning, but it's really wonderful. Haloumi is an unusual tasting cheese. It's a bit like feta but not as strong tasting. Made from sheeps' milk, it is not as strong as goats' milk cheese which I find a bit overpowering, but I know many people love it. Anyway, haloumi is quite delicate so it sits well with the egg. I hadn't tried it before making this dish, but I'm sold and frying it is fantastic.

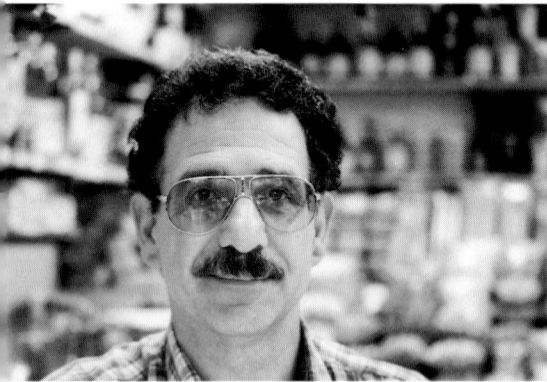

Haloumi Cheese

haloumi cheese

plain flour

olive oil

lemon juice

Break or slice the cheese into pieces, then dip each segment into the flour to coat.

Heat the oil in a frying pan and when hot fry the cheese until golden brown. Serve hot with a squeeze of fresh lemon juice.

Pastitsio is a Greek version of lasagne, using macaroni instead of the flat pasta sheets used by Italians. This pastitsio is made with egg yolks in the bechamel sauce which gives it added creaminess. It's deliciously rich and the mint adds an interesting sweetness. Once it's prepared, it doesn't need long in the oven because all the ingredients are already cooked. Just heat it long enough for it to bubble and turn a golden brown on top and it's ready to be served with a Greek salad featuring lots of black olives and finely chopped fresh parsley.

Pastitsio

500 g mince meat

1 onion, diced

1 sprig fresh mint, finely chopped

salt and pepper

handful of soft breadcrumbs

500 g long thick macaroni (Misko #1 is perfect)

For the sauce:

1 cup plain flour, well sifted

125 g butter

3 eggs, separated

1 litre milk

2 cups haloumi cheese, grated

nutmeg

salt and pepper

Make a bechamel sauce by melting the butter in a pot. Slowly sift the flour into the butter as you stir continuously. Add a pinch of salt, then stir continuously for about a minute. I like to let the flour and butter cook for a moment before adding the milk so it cooks through and the sauce doesn't taste of uncooked flour. Very slowly add the milk, stirring the mixture constantly until you have a smooth paste. Stir in the nutmeg. Take off the heat and allow to cool for a few minutes. Beat the egg yolks and when the sauce has cooled add them along with a good handful of the cheese to the mixture. Mix well and put aside.

Fry the onions and the meat in some olive oil until cooked through.

Add the mint and a pinch of salt and lots of freshly ground black pepper. When cooked, remove from heat and put aside.

While the meat is frying, cook the macaroni in lots of salted boiling water. When cooked, drain the macaroni and rinse in cold running water. Shake dry, then put about three-quarters of the macaroni into a large bowl and set the remaining pasta aside.

Grease a large baking dish, then sprinkle it with homemade soft breadcrumbs.

Beat the eggwhites until stiff and put aside. Add half of the meat mixture, half the remaining cheese, the beaten eggwhites and half of the sauce to the bowl in which you put most of the macaroni. Mix through to combine then spread it evenly over the breadcrumbs in the baking tin.

Next, spread the remaining meat mixture over the top of the combined mixture in the baking tin. Evenly lay the remaining macaroni over the top of the meat, then sprinkle with cheese. Spread the remaining sauce over the top, then sprinkle with more cheese.

Bake in a 250°C oven until golden brown.

Maria Laspina & Rosalinda Tasca

This mother and daughter team doesn't work at a market (although the produce from their family-run farm is sold to market stall holders) so, strictly speaking, they fall outside this book's parameters. But I wanted to include them anyway, not only because I had heard they were wonderful cooks, but because although they are once removed from the actual marketplace, they are involved behind the scenes as suppliers. Particularly though, they appear here because I wanted to make the connection between the land and the food we eat at our tables.

I think the connection in our minds between the land and our sustenance has been severed. Cucumbers are bought wrapped in plastic, unbrushed potatoes are frowned upon and eating from a box in front of the box has become not just a special treat at the end of a long day but a routine most nights of the week.

I was amazed as I drove through a town on my way to Adelaide via the Hay Plains to see a field of plants that reminded me of a toy I used to play with as a child. The toy, called clinkers if I remember properly, had two balls like snooker balls attached to the ends of a string which we held in the middle so the balls would strike together and bounce apart again. This field was like an inverted version of those balls. Instead of hanging down, stalks came up out of the ground at 45 degree angles and on top of them sat almost perfectly round balls. I had never seen anything like it before so I asked about it, describing what I'd seen, and someone told me they were garlic fields. I couldn't believe I had gone through my life without seeing garlic fields before and I wondered whether my son believes cucumbers grow in plastic wrap.

The LaSpinas originally came from Sicily but now live on a large property in Victoria's lush King Valley. The area was once almost solely devoted to the growing of tobacco crops yet now it is far more diverse. Like the LaSpinas, many people in the region have branched out into growing other crops, and for some who already had small vineyards used to make wine for personal consumption, it seemed like a natural progression to extend the vines and the production of wine.

This is a very picturesque part of the country and now host to a wine festival where all the local vineyards open their doors or, as is often the case, their sheds to the public for tastings. Word is that this area will become one for wine buffs to watch in the future. What were once small family vineyards are expanding at quite a rate and some have already been bought out by large commercial vignerons.

The LaSpina family realised the need to diversify their crops and move away from tobacco but they chose not to venture into grapes. They planted acres and acres of capsicums, tomatoes and even a kiwi fruit grove. They tried to make olive oil, which Maria explained to me 'is special to us — as children we helped our parents harvest our olive crop in Italy. We took the olives to our local mill and watched them be crushed between, what seemed to us as children, two huge round boulders. The juice which would then become the olive oil poured out one end and then all the stones and flesh would come out the other. At the end of the day, we'd take it all back home. The oil we cooked with, and the stones and the pulp we'd use to light our fire.

'We planted our own olive grove because we really wanted to make our own oil here, just like we did at home, but it didn't work out because there were no mills to do the crushing and the outlay to buy our own was too costly.' Maria speaks quite sadly when she talks about the olives and although most of the trees still stand on the property, the disappointment she felt at being unable to harvest the crops for oil dripped from her voice like the juice between the two boulders she so fondly remembered seeing as a child. The olives, I realised, were to be a real connection for the LaSpinas to their life back in Italy.

There is something powerful about trees that connects us to our homes. I remember a friend telling me about his trip to Japan and how surprised he was to visit a place that was heavy with the smell of eucalyptus. I wondered if, like these olive trees, the person who had planted those eucalypts in Japan somehow had with them a piece of their home, and with it a million memories tied up in the boughs of those swaying branches.

I thought about the olive grove that had been planted in the Adelaide foothills by an Italian migrant who moved there over a hundred years ago. He had left his country but brought with him, in those small seeds, one of the quintessential parts of his past to link him with his home.

Maria gave me this recipe after telling me about the olives because it features the strong flavour of virgin olive oil. These artichokes stuffed with garlic and rich with olive oil are perfect as part of an antipasto or served with salad and crusty fresh bread.

Maria's Roasted Artichokes

6 fresh artichokes

olive oil

Filling:

large handful of fresh mint, finely chopped

large handful of fresh parsley, finely chopped

1 bulb of peeled garlic cloves, crushed

$\frac{1}{2}$ teaspoon ground chilli

$\frac{1}{2}$ cup grated pecorino cheese

Wash the artichokes carefully in cold water. Peel off the tough outer layer of leaves. Turn the artichoke upside down and hit it against the chopping board to open out the leaves.

Combine all the ingredients for the filling in a bowl then divide the mixture evenly between the six artichokes. Pack the filling in between the leaves carefully, taking care not to break the artichokes.

Sit the artichokes in a baking dish and drizzle a tablespoon of olive oil onto each artichoke. Pour a cup of water into the baking dish and cover with foil.

Bake in a hot oven until cooked. The baking time will vary depending on how big the artichokes are, so test them by tugging at the leaves. If they come away easily, they are done; if they are hard to pull, place back in the oven and cook until tender.

The following

recipe of Maria's

is truly Italian —

it's another way

to make use of

all that not-quite-

fresh white bread

left over after

an authentic

Italian meal.

Spaghetti with Breadcrumbs

2 cups fresh homemade breadcrumbs

2 cloves garlic, crushed

1 cup olive oil

$\frac{1}{4}$ cup anchovy fillets

1 bunch wild fennel, finely chopped

$\frac{1}{2}$ cup slivered sun-dried tomatoes

salt and freshly ground black pepper

Make the breadcrumbs with day-old white bread. In a heavy-based pan, fry the garlic in the oil and add the anchovies. With a wooden spoon, stir the mixture and break up the anchovies as they cook through. Add the breadcrumbs and fry until golden. Toss in the fennel and add the sun-dried tomatoes and cook through. Season to taste, but remember the anchovies already will make this dish quite salty.

Meanwhile, cook enough spaghetti for six people in lots of boiling, lightly salted water, until al dente. When the spaghetti is cooked, scoop out a cup of the water in which it has been boiled and set aside. Drain the pasta well, then add it to the pan of breadcrumbs. Stir well to combine and if the mixture is a little dry add the water from the pasta and stir through.

Serve with lots of crusty bread, too fresh to use as crumbs and enjoy. The wild fennel really makes this dish, but if it is not available you could substitute a bunch of Italian parsley, though I suggest trying hard to find the fennel which is well worth the hunt.

The following marinated sardines need to be prepared at least 3 days in advance. They will keep for up to a week in the refrigerator but Maria challenges you to let them sit in your fridge once they are ready, as you'll be desperate to devour them with lashings of crusty bread. Be sure to serve the marinade with the sardines and suggest your guests drench their bread in the wonderful juice. The sardines will taste better if they are taken out of the fridge a little before serving so they are at room temperature when eaten.

Maria's Marinated Sardines

½ kg fresh sardines

wine vinegar

crushed garlic

1 handful fresh Italian parsley, finely chopped

1 cup chopped peperoncino (hot chilli)

olive oil

Gut, clean and wash the sardines. Remove the backbone from each fish and place in a glass baking dish or similar. Sprinkle with salt and cover in wine vinegar. Cover the dish with plastic wrap and place in the refrigerator for 2 days.

After the 2 days in the fridge, drain and discard the vinegar. In a separate bowl, combine all the other ingredients, then place a layer of sardines in the original marinating bowl and cover with some of the mixture. Place another layer of sardines on top, then cover with the other ingredients. Continue to layer until all the fish and mixture are used up.

Cover the fish with good quality olive oil and return to the fridge to marinate further for at least another 24 hours. Serve as suggested on the previous page.

Sardines Agrodolce

If you buy sardines and can't bear to wait for the
marinade of Maria's previous recipe to take effect,
then here is an accelerated method that will let
you enjoy the sardines almost straight away.

½ kg fresh sardines

olive oil

plain flour

2 cloves of garlic, crushed

1 cup of wine vinegar

Italian parsley, finely chopped

Gut, scale and clean the sardines under cold running water. Pat dry with
kitchen towels then roll the sardines in a plate of flour to cover lightly.

Heat olive oil in a heavy-based frying pan then fry the sardines until
golden brown. When cooked remove the sardines from the pan and
place them in a glass dish. Fry the garlic in a clean pan with fresh oil until
golden then remove from heat and add the vinegar, swirling the pan as
the liquid is added. Be careful when doing this as it can tend to splatter.
Pour the hot vinegar mixture over the sardines and sprinkle them with
parsley. Leave to cool at room temperature and serve with crusty bread
and a green salad.

Nina Scott

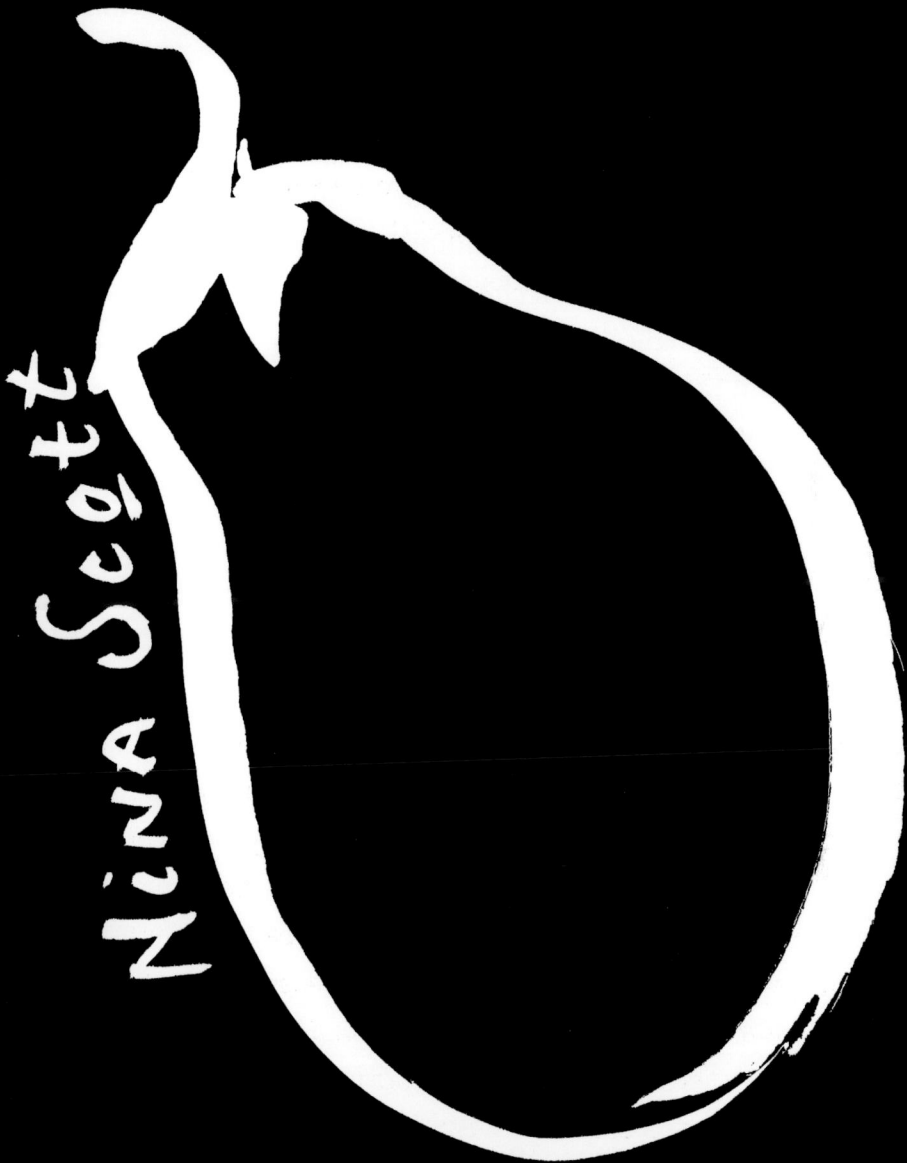

Fruit and Vegetable Section (Row B),
Victoria Markets

The Vic markets are huge and they are divided into sections. In the main building which fronts onto Elizabeth Street, only about 2 minutes from Melbourne's central business district, you will find all the delis and beside them, in another section, is all the meat and fish. Behind these two sections is where most of the fruit and vegetable stalls stand. At the back of the fruit and vegetables, across a quiet street which is filled with amusement rides and kids' farms on the weekend, you can find hundreds of clothing and general stalls selling everything from cheap watches to books and shoes. For a long time I thought the first two parts of the market were the only places to find foodstuffs, but one day I stumbled upon Nina and her brothers alongside the clothes stalls, selling fruit and vegetables. So if you're at the Vic markets, looking for things to cook for dinner, be sure to take a walk to Row B and see what's on offer over there.

It is a very long-standing tradition that Grecians never drink alcohol on its own. Since ancient times, *mezethes* (appetisers) have been served with alcohol. *Mezethes* can be anything as simple as a few olives and bread or more substantial like Nina's cheese triangles.

Cheese Triangles

These triangles are a great start to a dinner party, served with drinks, but be warned they're rich and quite filling. I enjoy them cold too, although admit they are especially wonderful served piping hot from the oven.

If you're planning a picnic these are excellent to take along, especially if you make them the morning you go so they're still warm when served with lots of crusty bread, black olives and green salad. If you're in a hurry, you can pre-prepare the filling as long as you store it in the fridge.

When I make cheese 'triangles', they're often served as squares or more usually strange shapes with little resemblance to their name. Cheese octangles or circles, perhaps. Here though, Nina explains very clearly just how to get the shape right.

For the filling:

1 tablespoon butter

1½ tablespoons plain flour

½ cup milk

125 g fetta cheese

60 g tasty cheese, grated

1 egg, beaten

2 tablespoons chopped parsley

¼ teaspoon ground nutmeg

pepper

Melt the butter, stir in the flour and cook gently on a low flame for about a minute. Slowly add the milk and stir continuously until mixture thickens and is smooth in texture. Take off heat and put aside to cool.

In a separate bowl, crumble the fetta with the grated tasty cheese. Stir in the beaten egg, the parsley, the nutmeg and the pepper to taste. When combined, stir in the milk and flour mixture. Mix gently, but ensure all ingredients are well combined.

For the case:

550 g filo pastry

¼ cup melted butter

Cut each filo sheet into three strips (approx. 13 x 30 cm). Stack the strips and quickly cover them with a dry cloth then with a dampened one so they won't become dry.

Lay a filo strip on a clean dry workbench and brush it lightly with the melted butter. Be sure to put the cover back over the remaining strips while you work or they will dry out and crack when folding.

To shape triangles:

Fold the strip in half lengthways and brush again with the butter. Place a portion (about a tablespoon, remembering the egg will make it puff up a bit) of filling on one end of the strip.

Fold the corner of the pastry over the filling to the folded edge of the filo and it will form a triangle. Continue to fold in triangles to the end of the strip and place seam-side down on a lightly greased baking tray. Brush the top with more melted butter and when all the strips and mixture have been made into triangles, place them in a moderate oven for 15–20 minutes until puffy and golden brown.

Nina warns the following recipe makes a large cake, so if you're wanting to feed lots of people it's perfect, otherwise halve the quantities. The sweet syrup, poured over and absorbed into the cake, makes this recipe wonderfully moist. Delicious with coffee.

Nina's Continental Semolina Cake

230 g (8 oz) butter

2 cups sugar

6 eggs

½ cup milk

3 cups semolina

2 cups self-raising flour

1 cup blanched chopped almonds

a little lemon rind if liked

a few extra blanched almonds, halved, for decoration

Syrup:

5 cups sugar

6 cups water

a few drops lemon juice

Beat butter and sugar to a cream, adding eggs one at a time. When smooth, add the lemon peel (if used) and the almonds. Mix well. Add some semolina, some flour and then some milk alternately, repeating till all the ingredients are used. When well combined, pour the mixture into a prepared baking dish about 25 x 30 cms. Decorate the top with some halved blanched almonds. Bake in a moderate oven for about an hour, or until cake is cooked through and golden on top.

While the cake is cooking make a syrup by boiling the sugar, water and lemon juice and stirring until reduced to a syrup-like consistency. Take off heat and leave to cool.

When the cake is cooked, remove it from the oven and pour the cooled syrup over the top while it's still in the tin. Allow to cool before removing and slicing.

The acidity of
the marinade in
the following
recipe makes for
wonderfully tender
meat. If you use
bamboo skewers,
soak them in water
for a few hours
before threading
them with the meat.
If the skewers are
dry, they will catch
and burn, so it's
wise to soak them.

Skewered Lamb

1 leg of lamb about 2 kg, boned

½ cup olive oil

½ cup dry white wine

juice of one or two lemons

rigani

2 cloves garlic, crushed

salt and pepper

Cut the lamb into 4 cm cubes and place in a dish. Add the remaining ingredients to the bowl of lamb and stir to coat the meat well in the marinade. Cover and refrigerate for at least 12, but preferably 24, hours. Stir the meat occasionally while it marinates.

Lift the meat from the marinade and reserve the liquid for basting. Thread the meat onto metal or bamboo skewers. Cook under a hot grill or over glowing charcoals on the barbecue. Baste the meat with the marinade while cooking. Cook the meat as desired, remembering the traditional Greek method would cook the meat very well.

When cooked, place the skewers on a bed of boiled rice garnished with parsley and wedges of lemon. Accompany with a fresh green or Greek salad.

Nina makes this dip to be served as a *mezethes,* all by hand, as it would have been done traditionally. The result is a smooth but textured dip. It can be made in a blender and the result is very smooth but not so authentic. If you are doing it in a blender, cook the eggplant as directed below, but then place all the ingredients except the oil in the mixer. Whirl on a slow speed until smooth and then increase the speed, while gradually adding the oil.

Remember that eggplant discolours very quickly in the open air, so once they're peeled, be sure to make the dip quickly. If, for any reason, you can't make the dip as soon as the eggplants are peeled, squeeze lemon juice over the flesh to stop discolouration.

Eggplant Dip

1 large or 2 medium oval eggplants (about 500 g)

1 clove garlic

salt

$^3/_4$ cup fresh soft white breadcrumbs

3 tablespoons lemon juice

$^1/_2$ cup olive oil

1 small onion, grated

2 tablespoons chopped parsley

freshly ground black pepper

Place the whole eggplants, unpeeled, on a baking tray and cook in a moderate oven for between 30 and 50 minutes, depending on size. They should be soft to the touch when they're ready. Remove from oven and while still hot remove the skin and chop the flesh up roughly.

Crush the garlic with $^1/_2$ teaspoon of salt in a large bowl. Gradually add the warm eggplant to the bowl, alternating with the soft breadcrumbs. Slowly add the lemon juice and the olive oil while stirring to mix thoroughly. Stir in the onion, the parsley and some more salt to taste, along with fresh pepper.

Put the mixture in a serving bowl and refrigerate. The mixture will thicken as it cools. When cool and thick, serve garnished with black olives and crusty bread.

Nina's Stuffing for Lamb or Chicken

Nina says her family can't get enough of this stuffing, which, she admits, 'is very, very nice'.

1 medium onion, finely chopped

3 rashers bacon, finely chopped

3 cups fresh breadcrumbs

1 teaspoon dried rigani

2 tablespoons olive oil

Saute the onion in the olive oil until transparent, add the bacon and cook through gently. Put the breadcrumbs in a bowl, then add the onions and the bacon when they're cooked. Add the rigani and stir the mixture while gradually adding the olive oil left over from the frying.

When well combined, pack the stuffing into the meat before roasting.

Connie & Alfonso Rotolo

Athens Gourmet Food,
Central Market, Adelaide

Connie and Alfonso ran the Athens delicatessen for many years. Shortly before I arrived in Adelaide to research this book they sold the shop and were sadly preparing themselves for their last weeks behind the counter. So, when I spoke to them about being in this book they were thrilled because they thought it would be a great reminder of all their happy years at the Central Market. Connie and Alfonso had created a wonderful deli that brimmed with gourmet delights and it was with some sadness that, the next time I went to Adelaide, I looked in vain for their smiling faces behind the counter.

For most of the people I spoke to in relation to this book, I had no particular recipes in mind. If I thought I was particularly lacking in a culinary area I might guide them loosely towards it, but Connie was different. Someone had told me they had tried Connie's panforte and it was truly to die for. So when I introduced myself to Connie and she asked me what kind of thing I was after, I said, 'Well, I've heard you make the best panforte in town and I'd love your recipe for that.' Connie looked embarrassed at the praise and worked out who we both knew who could have told me about her secret talents — she swore she'd kill them.

I could tell Connie's panforte was special, not only for those who ate it, but for her too. When her recipes arrived by post, she apologised there was no panforte recipe — she couldn't bring herself to divulge her secret family method — but instead she included another of her specialties, pastiera napoletana, in its place. If these recipes are anything to go by, I can imagine just how good her panforte must be and only wish I'd got to taste it myself.

Panna Cotta

This panna cotta is very rich so you won't need to serve large amounts. I love dipping into this sweet, creamy dessert with almond bread or biscuits, using the bread almost like a spoon. Panna cotta is very similar to blancmange and I love the way it wobbles jelly-like on the plate. It looks great served with a selection of fresh berries brimming from its centre, and the acidity of the berries cuts down some of the richness of this dessert.

600 ml double cream

4 tablespoons sugar, or a little less depending on taste

1 teaspoon vanilla extract

2 teaspoons gelatin

On a very low heat, simmer the cream with the sugar and vanilla for 2–3 minutes. In a cup, dissolve the gelatin in 2 tablespoons of cold water. Be careful not to add extra gelatin or your dessert will be rubbery. Once the gelatin is dissolved, beat the mixture into the cream very thoroughly.

Pour the mixture into a ring mould and chill for a few hours. If the panna cotta is not refrigerated for long enough it will be too runny to keep its shape, so ensure you leave plenty of time before serving for it to set properly. To remove the panna cotta from the ring mould, tip it upside down on a plate. If you have trouble shaking it out, you can run the bottom of the mould very quickly under a warm tap, taking care just to wet the mould, not the dessert. Fill with a selection of fresh berries and serve.

This recipe will only fill a smallish ring-mould pan, so if you are wanting to serve a lot of people and want to have a large hole in which to put the berries, perhaps double the recipe. Remember though that this is very rich and usually only small servings will be eaten.

It's not surprising when you consider the similarities between pizza and pasta to learn that they both originated in the south of Italy where the weather is perfect for wheat growing. Making pizza dough was a natural extension of making bread. Initially just olives and herbs were added to the dough but the concept of adding other ingredients slowly evolved over the years to create the pizza we know today.

Fast Pizza Napoletana

Tomato base:

1 kg fresh ripe tomatoes

3 cloves garlic

$\frac{1}{4}$ cup extra virgin olive oil

origano

salt and a little sugar

Put all the topping ingredients in a pan and cook on a low heat until reduced — about 20 minutes. A little sugar is sometimes used to deflect the sharpness of the tomatoes. Generally I find that if you use fresh ripe tomatoes, the sugar is unnecessary. When using canned tomatoes, on the other hand, the sugar may be a necessary addition because the tomatoes tend not to be sweet or terribly flavoursome.

While the tomato base is cooking, make this pizza dough.

Pizza dough:

5 cups of strong flour

1 heaped tablespoon Fermipan yeast

salt

warm water

In a large mixing bowl, place flour, yeast, salt and mix well. Add water slowly while mixing to form a firm, sticky dough. Remove the dough from the bowl and place on a clean dry, lightly floured surface. Knead the dough by hand for about 10 minutes until it is smooth and elastic.

Separate the dough into three pieces, then roll each one out into a circle with a rolling pin smeared in olive oil until thin.

Place the rolled out dough on an oiled baking tray and spread the tomato base then the topping out evenly over the three rounds.

Pizza topping:

fresh bocconcini slices

grated Italian parmigiano

fresh basil leaves

extra virgin olive oil

Let the pizzas sit at room temperature for about 30 minutes while the yeast rises. Bake in a hot oven until golden brown.

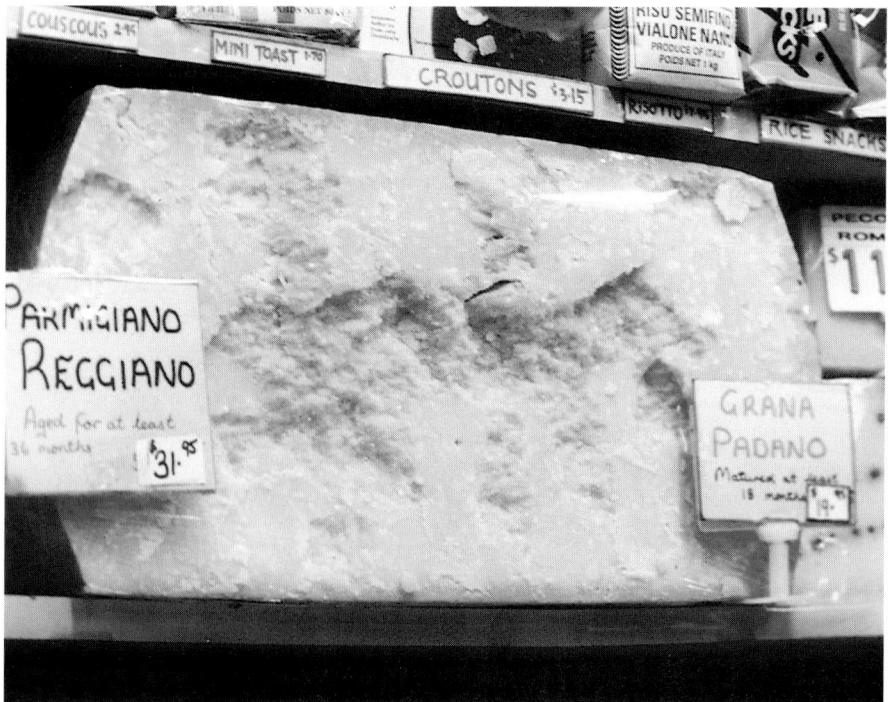

Asparagi sotto Olio

(Asparagus preserved in extra virgin olive oil)

Asparagus is not a cheap vegetable at the best of times. If you are buying it out of season then the price can be prohibitive. So here is a recipe you can make at the height of the season when the prices are low which will ensure you have the perfect accompaniment to your antipasto all through the year.

500 ml red wine vinegar

500 ml water

salt

extra virgin olive oil

5 bunches asparagus

sterilised jars

Break the tough dry bottoms off the asparagus. Wash the asparagus well to remove any dirt. In a large pot, bring the water, salt and vinegar to the boil. When really bubbling, add the asparagus and cook for about 5 minutes until tender but still nice and crisp. Drain and plunge into cold water to prevent further cooking. Gently lay the asparagus spears on clean tea-towels for about 6–8 hours until they are completely dry.

Pack the spears tightly into sterilised jars. Cover the asparagus with good quality oil, seal the jars tightly and store in the fridge for up to a year.

If you take any spears from the jar, be sure to use clean utensils or you risk losing your whole jar to mould. All preserves need to be covered in oil, so keep an eye on the levels and top up with extra oil as necessary or use a weight to keep the preserved produce submerged.

Both potatoes and tomatoes feature heavily in Italian cooking. Here is a great side dish (*contorno*) recipe using these staples that is perfect to accompany a roast or just about any other main meal that calls for vegetables on the side.

Patate e Pomodori

1 kg potatoes

1 kg ripe tomatoes

garlic, crushed

finely chopped Italian parsley

homemade chicken stock

extra virgin olive oil

salt and freshly ground black pepper

Peel potatoes and slice them into rounds about ½ cm thick. Slice tomatoes slightly more thickly and in a heavy baking pan lay slices of potato and slices of tomato in adjacent rows.

Mix the remaining ingredients with the olive oil and a little water or stock. Drizzle this mixture over the potatoes and the tomatoes.

Bake at 190°C for about 40 minutes until the potatoes are tender and soft when pricked with a fork.

Leftover *contorno* can be used as the basis for a wonderful frittata. The frittata can be served hot or cold for lunch or as an addition to an antipasto. It's great to take on a picnic. All you need to do is break 6 to 8 eggs into a bowl, depending on how many portions you wish to serve. (Six eggs will make enough frittata for 4 people.)

Beat the eggs well and add a handful each of freshly chopped basil and Italian parsley. Grind in lots of black pepper and salt to taste. Set aside.

Frittata is quite sweet and it is the onions that make it that way, so use quite a few. Gently fry about 4 onions in a little olive oil until transparent.

If you have any leftover *contorno*, add it to the frying pan and heat through. If you are starting from scratch, chop 4 large ripe tomatoes and add them to the onions. Slices of zucchini can be added as well as green or red capsicum — really you can use just about any vegetable for a frittata. If you like ham, thin strips can be added to the frypan of vegetables as well. Gently fry all the vegetables (and ham if used) until tender.

Pour the egg and herb mixture over the vegetables, cover the pan with a lid and make sure the heat is very low. Like an omelette, this shouldn't be stirred. After a minute, sprinkle in a couple of handfuls of freshly shaved parmigiano cheese and put the lid back on. Cook with the lid on for another 3 or 4 minutes then remove the pan from the flame. Take the lid off and slide the pan in under a hot grill for another few minutes, until the frittata is golden. Remove from pan and serve with salad. (Be careful if you are using a plastic handled pan that it doesn't melt under the grill.)

GNOCCHI
PUMPKIN

$9.00
Kg.

SPECIAL

AUOLi
~ Pumpkin
cotta.

$11.95

Connie serves this salad as an antipasto. It makes a pleasant change from Caesar salad and Connie's warm dressing gives it a special twist.

The salad can be washed and drained several hours ahead of time if you then cover and refrigerate it. The dressing can also be made in advance and left at room temperature but you will need to reheat it just before serving.

Green Salad with Prosciutto and Warm Balsamic Dressing

1 Spanish onion, thinly sliced into rings

$^1/_2$ cup sherry vinegar (Spanish if possible)

1 small head each of cos, radicchio, endive and some rocket

$^1/_2$ cup roasted pine nuts

5 shallots, sliced

100 g parmigiano cheese, shaved

100 g thinly sliced prosciutto, cut into squares

1 cup fresh basil leaves

1 cup fresh Italian parsley

Dressing

10 cloves garlic, diced into quarters

$^2/_3$ cup extra virgin olive oil

8 tablespoons balsamic vinegar

3 tablespoons red wine vinegar

1 tablespoon brown sugar

salt and pepper to taste

Assembling the salad: Soak the onions in $^1/_2$ cup of vinegar for 30 minutes. Tear the leaves into bite-sized pieces and place in a large bowl. Toss the greens with all but a few of the pine nuts, most of the shallots, half the cheese, half the prosciutto and all the basil and parsley. Arrange on a large platter.

Making the dressing: In a medium skillet slowly cook the garlic in the olive oil over a low heat for about 5–6 minutes. Remove with a slotted spoon and reserve. Turn the heat to medium-high and add the vinegars to the oil. Cook for a few moments until the acid has diffused slightly. Add brown sugar to taste and let the mixture bubble slowly for 1 minute. Taste for sweet/tart balance. Take care to cool the mixture as the oil will make the dressing scorching hot. If the dressing is too sweet, stir in extra balsamic vinegar to taste. Simmer for a few minutes to boil off some of the acid from the vinegar. Stir in reserved garlic and season with salt and pepper. Set aside until ready to serve.

To serve: Top the salad platter with the drained red onions and scatter the rest of the shallots, pine nuts, cheese and prosciutto over the salad. Reheat the dressing, stirring vigorously to blend and then spoon over the salad.

Blanched asparagus and slices of avocado and a few black olives can be added on top once the salad is dressed.

Italians use bread almost like an eating utensil and this dish would be served with a crusty loaf which would be broken up and dipped into the delicious dressing.

Aceto di vino

SA Ho
Artichoke
L $

Aceto Di
d White

This is the recipe Connie sent in place of her panforte. As soon as I read through this I didn't mind forgoing the panforte (which I sometimes find a bit too sweet), as for me this recipe wins hands down. It is another lattice-topped pie, along the lines of the recipe from Cyril's (see page 123) but this time it's filled not with jam but with sweet ricotta and rice which combine to make a delicate rice custard filling.

This recipe reminded me a little of the rice pudding my grandmother used to make me when I was growing up. Really though, it's just the creamy rice that bears any resemblance to this dish which is flavoured with liquor and citron.

Citron is preserved lemon which is very expensive to buy here in Australia. If you're making this for a special occasion, it's worth the expense to include citron. Otherwise you can use grated lemon or lime peel and a bit of glacé orange (not the really sweet syrupy kind).

In Italy, around Easter time, you will see many dishes like this one which feature the fresh cheese, ricotta. Italians were quick to notice the difference in their dairy produce during the spring when the pastures are particularly green and lush, resulting in a noticeably richer, creamier, sweeter milk. It makes sense to feature the enhanced flavours at this time of year when they are readily available.

Pastiera Napoletana

(Easter Rice and Ricotta Cake)

Pastry:

125 g butter

125 g castor sugar

2 egg yolks

250 g strong flour (the kind used for
making pasta rather than cake flour)

vanilla extract

rind of 1 lemon, grated

Rub the butter into the flour, sugar, vanilla and lemon rind. Add the egg
yolks. Mix well and knead until smooth and soft. If the dough is too dry
add a little water or milk or even more egg.

Eggs vary a great deal in their size and therefore the moisture they
add to the mixture. As with making spaghetti, you will have to use your
judgment and don't worry if your mixture needs an extra egg. When I
made this dough, I added another egg as well as some milk because the
mixture was too dry at first.

Once the dough is the right consistency, let it rest.

Filling:

500 g ricotta

150–200 g sugar

lemon rind and juice

100 g candied citron (available from good delicatessens)

6 eggs

700 ml milk

1 cup arborio rice (short grained
rice, used most often in risotto)

1 vanilla bean

Strega Liquore

Make a rice custard by bringing the milk to the boil, making sure you stir it often. Add the split vanilla bean and the rice. Cook very slowly until the rice is tender. Add more milk if needed. Let cool.

Cream the ricotta with the sugar, lemon rind, eggs, vanilla extract and Strega Liquore to taste. Remove the vanilla bean from the rice and add the rice custard and the chopped citron to the ricotta mixture. Mix well.

Roll out two-thirds of the pastry and lay it on a prepared 23–25 cm spring-form cake tin. Press the pastry into the base of the mould and round the sides. Pour in the filling. Roll out the rest of the pastry and add more flour to make a slightly firmer dough. Cut into long strips and arrange the strips to form a lattice on top of the filling. Brush the top with milk or egg yolk and bake at 180°C for about 55 minutes or until golden brown.

Bill trimas

Victoria Markets

Bill runs a tiny stall in the deli section of the Vic markets. Despite its size it's a great place to find delicious dips, cheeses and olives. Bill was born in Australia but the following is a very traditional Greek recipe often served in his home.

I had made tzatziki before
meeting Bill but not by his
method. In the past I had
salted the cucumber to extract
the water and used yoghurt
just as it came from the tub.
Bill's method makes a thicker
creamier dip and the result
is much better.

Tzatziki

(Yoghurt Dip)

1 kg natural yoghurt

1 long cucumber

salt

olive oil

6 cloves garlic, crushed

Put the yoghurt in a calico bag or a clean pillowcase and hang it over a bowl or the sink overnight so all the water drains through the cloth.

With a vegetable peeler, peel the skin from the cucumber and discard. Hold the cucumber in your hand and continue to peel long strips of the flesh until it is all shredded. With your hands, squeeze the peelings tightly to extract some of the water.

Pour the drained yoghurt, which should be quite thick now, into a bowl and add the cucumber peelings, some salt and the garlic. Mix well or blend quickly for only a few seconds in a food processor.

Serve with crusty bread and black olives as part of a *mezethes* or use the dip to accompany barbecued lamb skewers as part of a main course.

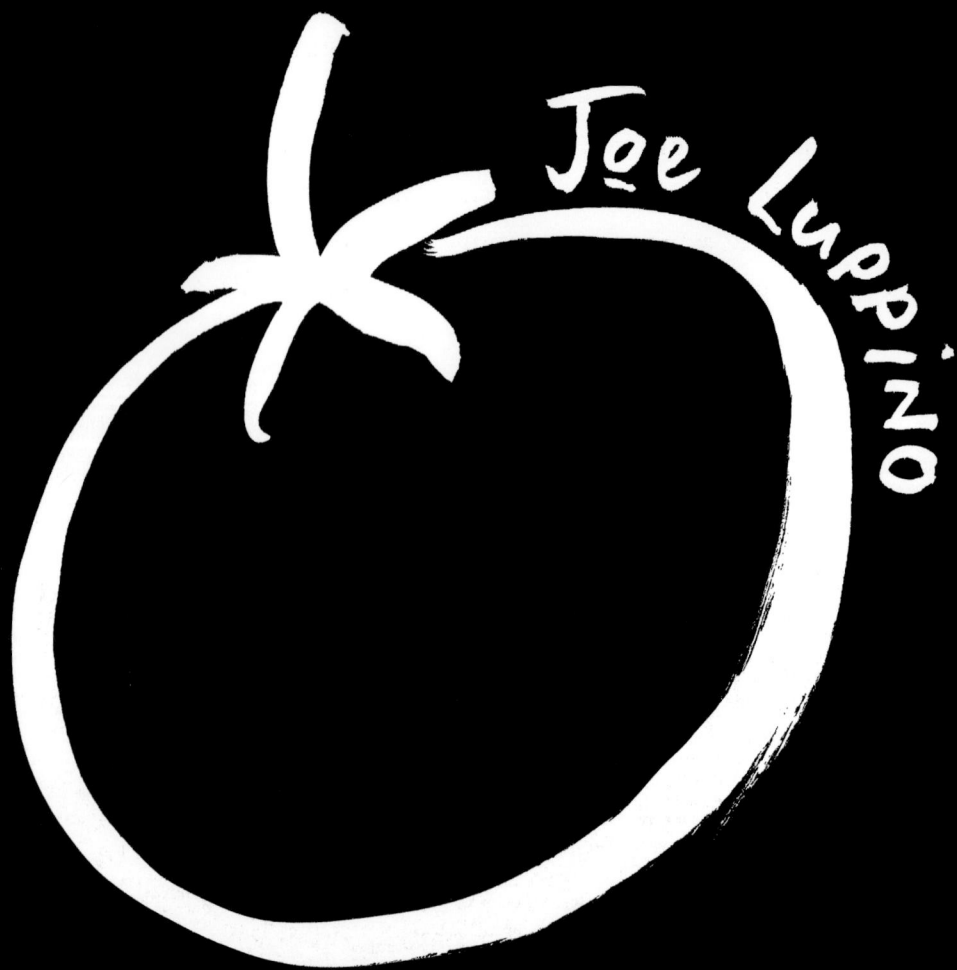

Joe Luppino

Port Adelaide Market

Joe is one of many characters at the Port market. Often I went to his stall to find boxes and boxes of tomatoes, but no Joe.

I would look around, wondering where he'd gone and more often than not he'd be over with the men who sell salami from the back of their panel van, having a chat. Especially if it were terribly hot, he'd be there, sharing the shade of their umbrella, keeping an eye on his stall from a place out of the sun.

One of the things you soon realise about the markets is that although all the stall holders are in competition with one another, there is a great sense of community there. For many of the sellers, it's just as much a social occasion as a serious day's work.

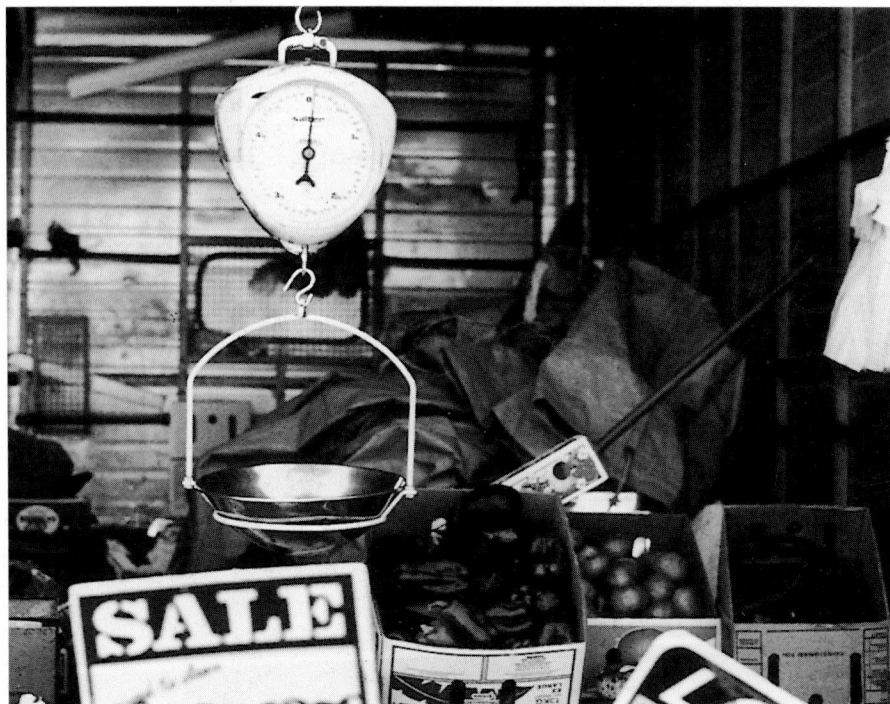

Minestrone is a heavy soup, perhaps the most common and well-known peasant dish from Italy. This recipe uses three kinds of pulses and, like many other peasant dishes, it features strong-tasting olive oil to add fragrance and flavour to the dish. Recipes for minestrone vary a little depending on who you talk to and which region they are from. The point that all Italians agree upon no matter where they were born is that when the minestrone is served, a large drizzle of olive oil must be added to the individual bowls. That it must also be accompanied by a very fresh loaf of crusty bread and shavings of fresh parmigiano goes without saying. One quite different alternative I did hear about is that in some regions minestrone is served with a dollop of pesto.

Often the water in which the beans are cooked is discarded and fresh water used as the basis for the soup. In this recipe, Joe uses the water in which the beans have been soaked for the soup but makes sure he rinses the beans thoroughly to remove any grit before they are boiled.

Minestrone

²/₃ cup borlotti beans

²/₃ cup cannellini beans

²/₃ cup chick peas

1 onion

3 ripe tomatoes

2 sticks celery

2 potatoes

basil

olive oil

salt

250 g ditoloni pasta
(cube-shaped)

Half fill a large saucepan with tepid water and add all the rinsed beans. Bring to the boil and simmer for 1½ hours. Let stand.

Fry the chopped onion in olive oil until transparent. Add the chopped tomatoes, basil and salt and saute until well cooked (about 15 minutes). Remove from heat.

Chop the celery, carrots and the potatoes.

Place the pan of beans back on the stove. When they return to the boil, add the cooked tomato mixture and the chopped vegetables and cook for about 15 minutes. Add the pasta and stir often so it separates, until cooked. Add 1 scoop (about a dessert spoon) of olive oil and stir. Remove from heat and let stand for 5 minutes before serving as suggested above.

Tomatoes are a feature of Joe's stall. He does also sell other vegetables but tomatoes are his speciality. You can buy boxes of green tomatoes for chutney and firm red romas for salads as well as very ripe specimens for tomato sauce or soups. When I talked to stall owners, I usually asked them to give me recipes featuring the foods they sold on their stalls. Joe had already given me his minestrone recipe, but the next time I was down at the port he chased me through the crowd of Sunday morning shoppers clutching this recipe for tomato sauce for spaghetti.

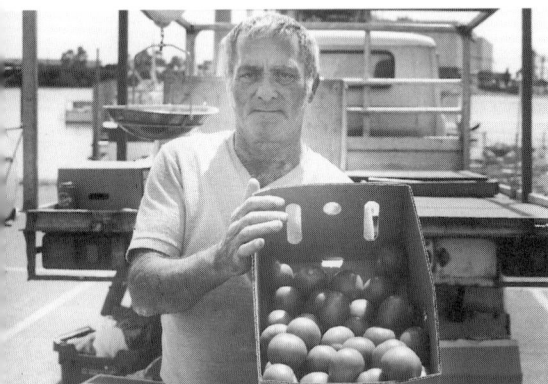

Spaghetti with Fresh Tomatoes

2 kg ripe tomatoes

1 onion

olive oil

basil

salt

origano

pinch hot dried chilli

500 g spaghetti

parmigiano or pecorino cheese, grated

Fry the chopped onion in olive oil until it is transparent. When onions are cooked slowly they release their natural sugars and the resulting sauce will be improved with the extra sweet flavour. Add the chopped tomatoes, salt, basil, origano and hot chilli to taste. Simmer for 30 minutes to allow the flavours to mingle and the tomato juice to evaporate.

Cook the spaghetti until it is firm. Drain the pasta then add it to the tomato mixture and cook on a high heat for 5 minutes. Serve with fresh basil leaves on the side of the plate.

Anna Nicolaidis

Deli Section, Victoria Markets

Anna Nicolaidis runs a wonderful deli at the Victoria markets where you can buy cheeses of just about any description. The day I saw her she was too busy to talk much, but she sent me the following recipes, written in Greek, by post.

This recipe uses canned artichoke hearts, which if you are in a hurry will suffice, but of course the fresh kind you prepare yourself will taste better, so here is a quick rundown on how to prepare the hearts for this dish.

Choose fresh bright-looking artichokes. Cut off the stem to within about an inch of the bulb. Put the artichokes in a large pot of boiling water to which you have added a splash of vinegar to stop any discolouration. Boil until tender then remove the leaves until the cap-shaped heart is exposed.

Artichoke Hearts and Potatoes

10 fresh artichoke hearts or 2 cans artichoke hearts

2 onions, grated

2–3 chopped carrots

2–3 potatoes, sliced thickly

juice of half a lemon

olive oil

water

Place the onions and the carrots along with the slices of potato in a saucepan. Cover with water, the juice from the artichoke hearts and a good splash of oil. If you are using fresh hearts, you will need to add more oil and perhaps a dash of vinegar (not too much though) to maintain the liquid level. Cook for 1 hour, then add the artichokes and the lemon juice and cook for a further half hour.

Serve with a Greek salad and fresh crusty bread dipped into the sauce.

Usually Anna's keftedes meatballs are served as part of a *mezethes*, although they can be served with side vegetables if you want to make more of a substantial meal from them, or with a Greek salad and fresh bread for a lighter alternative. Whichever way, they are quite delicious and the fresh mint gives them a wonderful sweet flavour.

Anna's Keftedes

(Meatballs)

1 kg lean mince meat

1 onion, grated

½ cup fresh breadcrumbs

2 eggs

salt and pepper

sprig of fresh mint, chopped finely

sprig of fresh rigani, chopped finely

handful of freshly chopped flat leaf parsley

2 tablespoons vinegar

plain flour

Place all the ingredients except the flour in a bowl and knead them together until well combined. Cover and place in the fridge for a few hours.

Roll the mixture into small balls in the palm of your hand. Roll each ball in the flour so they are lightly coated. Heat some oil in a frying pan and then gently place a few balls in the hot oil. Don't put too many in at a time or they will break up and stick together. Cook until golden brown. Place the cooked balls on an ovenproof plate and put in a warm oven to keep hot while other balls are cooking.

The following dish is rather like a lasagne in that it has meat cooked in tomatoes then baked in the oven with pasta on top and served with lashings of grated cheese. This version uses the tiny pasta riso that looks exactly like rice but is made from wheat. Personally, I prefer this recipe to the traditional lasagne as it doesn't use a bechamel sauce which I find a bit daunting and heavy. This is a hearty meal, fantastic for winter.

Baked Beef
and Pasta

1 kg lean beef

olive oil

1 onion, grated

$\frac{1}{2}$ kg fresh ripe tomatoes, chopped

a spoonful of tomato paste

salt and pepper

1 bay leaf

2 cups pasta riso (which looks exactly like
rice and can be bought from good delis)

grated cheese

butter

Cut the beef into large bite-sized chunks. Heat a saucepan and seal the
beef, tossing until the juices evaporate. Add a dash of oil and the grated onion and stir until golden brown. Add the tomatoes and the paste,
stir through and simmer until the tomatoes are tender. Add enough
water to cover the beef and continue to simmer. Season with the salt
and pepper and add the bay leaf. Continue simmering until the meat is
tender and cooked through.

Remove from the stove and place in a baking dish. Sprinkle the pasta
over the top of the meat until it is covered with a good thick layer, so
you can't see the sauce. The pasta will cook in the juices of the meat mixture, so be careful not to add too much pasta or there won't be enough
liquid to cook it in. Place in a moderate oven until the pasta is cooked —
about 20 minutes — then remove from the oven, sprinkle with grated
cheese and serve with a dollop of butter or a splash of olive oil. Goes
well with a Greek salad with lots of Kalamata olives.

I had often seen okra in Asian grocery stores and always loved the look of it, but never bought any because I didn't know how to cook it, nor exactly what it went with. Some people call okra 'lady fingers', because it is long and slender. It has five sides that taper down to an elegant point with small seeds inside. Last year when I visited New York, I went to the famous deli, Dean and Deluca's, where I bought gumbo spices which I brought home for friends as a souvenir present. The next time I went to their house for dinner they cooked up the most wonderful seafood gumbo which I devoured and adored. They gave me their special recipe which of course features okra, so I now know a little about this fabulous vegetable.

Okra exudes a sticky juice which thickens the dishes it is cooked in to a smooth, almost jelly-like consistency. Some suggest salting the okra, like you do eggplant, before cooking it to remove some of this fluid. Maria's recipe uses canned okra — and it is a vegetable that does survive the canning process — so if you can't find it fresh, use a can. Be sure to rinse the okra well even when using the canned variety. If you want to use fresh okra, wash it well under cold water and dry thoroughly before cutting off the conical lid from the stalk end. Be careful not to cut too far and expose the seeds and inside flesh or it will fall apart during cooking. Either salt the okra and leave it to exude its juices for an hour before again rinsing well or soak it in about a litre of water to which you have added about 100 ml of vinegar for three-quarters of an hour. Either method will suffice.

Okra and Chicken

6 chicken drumsticks

1 grated onion

2 cloves garlic, crushed

olive oil

$^3/_4$ kg fresh ripe tomatoes, chopped

good pinch of salt

1 kg fresh okra (prepared as on previous page) or
2 cans of okra (well rinsed)

2 tablespoons of vinegar

Heat a good splash of olive oil in a saucepan. Brown the onion and the garlic before adding the drumsticks and cooking to a golden colour while stirring. Add the okra and on a fairly high heat brown it also. Add the tomatoes and turn the heat down to simmer for about 20 minutes until the chicken is cooked through and the okra is tender. Add a little water if the mixture is too dry, but only ever shake the pan gently to move the sauce around or the okra will break up and lose its lovely look. When the ingredients are cooked, add the vinegar, heat through and remove from heat.

   Serve on a bed of rice to soak up the rich thick juices and accompany with a Greek salad.

I always make huge salads and the following kind, which plays a very special part in many Greek meals, is one I think deserves to be featured. Unlike most salads that contain large amounts of lettuce, or similar greens, this one uses only a little lettuce, allowing the tomatoes and other ingredients to take their place at the centre of this Grecian stage.

Greek Salad

1/4 large lettuce, cut in ribbons

8–10 vine-ripened or roma tomatoes

cucumber about 15 cm long, peeled and sliced

1/2 white onion, cut in thin rings

sprigs of fresh mint

lots of Kalamata olives

250 g Greek feta cheese

juice of 1 lemon

extra virgin olive oil

sprigs of fresh or dried rigani

Layer a bowl or plate with the lettuce ribbons. Cut the tomatoes in long segments and place them around the plate or bowl. Toss in the slices of cucumber and grind some sea or rock salt over the top. Push the onion rounds into individual rings and scatter across the top. Chop up the feta into large chunks and toss it in with lots of good quality Kalamata olives. Rip up and scatter the mint and rigani if it is fresh or sprinkle the dried herbs over the top of the salad. Drizzle the lemon juice and extra virgin olive oil over the top, grind in fresh pepper and serve immediately or the cheese will dry out and the salad go limp.

Stocks are very important in Greek and Italian
cooking. A good stock will add richness and flavour
to dishes. It will deepen the taste and a fresh stock just
cannot be compared to a bought one or a cube. Often
wine is used as a substitute for stock but I find it adds
too much acidity to many dishes and the taste of the
wine dominates all others. Of course some dishes
require wine, but when it's used to add liquid to a dish
in the same way as stock, it doesn't work as well. If I'm
making a risotto I will buy a whole bird and make a
stock by cooking the bird using the method set out on
the following page. When the meat is ready, I remove
the bird from the pot, take the flesh from the bones,
then return the bones to the water. I then add the
chicken meat to the risotto and use the stock
for cooking.

Stock

1 whole chicken or 1 kg chicken bones

water

1 onion, peeled, but left whole

1 tomato, whole

2 carrots, cut in large chunks

1 bay leaf

2 stalks celery, cut in large chunks

freshly ground black pepper

Cut the fat from the chicken. I peel the skin off as well which is a gruelling job, but worth it for a rich but non-greasy stock. Put the chicken in a large pot and cover it in cold water. Add the whole tomato and onion, the chopped vegetables and the bay leaf along with lots of fresh pepper and some salt. Bring to the boil and then simmer until the meat is cooked. Take the bird from the pot and remove the flesh from the bones. Put the bones back in the pot and continue to simmer for at least an hour. Sometimes a greyish scum will form on top of the water — it should be removed with a spoon and discarded.

Use the meat in a risotto or it may be appropriate to use in the dish for which you are making your stock — use your judgment. (I often use the chicken in my son's school sandwiches.)

When the stock is ready, drain it through a colander with another pot underneath to catch the rich juice. Discard the vegetables and bones and use the stock as directed in the recipe.

Stock freezes really well, so if you make more than you need put it in a container in the freezer until the next time. Use a bit of fresh stock in a pasta or vegetable sauce and taste the difference.

Lucia

Lucia's Cafe   Central Market   Adelaide

Adelaide marketgoers will know Lucia's cafe. It has been an institution in Adelaide for many years and recently won an award for best coffee there. When I worked at the Central Markets, I was always running to Lucia's and ordering coffees in between sales. Lucia's was, and still is, the place to be on Saturday morning. When I worked at the markets, it was where everyone met after doing their shopping, moving tables and chairs (much to the dislike of Pasquale) and sitting deep in conversation or gossip, ordering coffee after coffee for hours on end. Lucia's is famous not only for its coffee — strong and, if you like cappuccino, they make the best froth — but also for its pizzas. In fact Lucia and her husband Pasquale were the first people to make and sell pizza in Australia. What is remarkable about Lucia's cafe is that she still makes everything 'home-style'. Lucia makes all the tomato sauce for the pizzas from fresh tomatoes she preserves herself. It is hard work, as this story written by her daughter Maria shows, but once you taste a pizza from Lucia's you will know it is well worth the effort. This story (and the recipes within it) give a window into the culture of a traditional Italian family, and seeps with the warmth and generosity Lucia's cafe is famous for.

Lucia loves her garden. It always amazes me the incredible energy she has which enables her to do so much.

At the moment in the garden there are at least 120 tomato plants full of beautiful fruit. The first harvest was done yesterday and tonight we are about to have spaghetti al pomodoro — oil, garlic, onion, tomato and lots of fresh basil, served with grated romano cheese and freshly ground black pepper.

As well as tomato, Lucia has a great variety of lettuce in her garden — cos, radicchio, arugula (rocket) and endive. She also grows garlic, Spanish onions, zucchini, potato, spinach, capsicum, beans and peas.

Always at this time of year Lucia has lots of basil, origano, thyme and parsley. Lucia grows enough basil and origano to use fresh as well as drying it for the winter months.

The tomatoes grown in her garden are for her own supply of tomato sauce which she makes for all the family — her two daughters Nicci and Maria, son-in-law John and her three grandchildren Lee, Simon and Emma.

However, sauce making and preserving do not stop there. For the cafe, the usual number of bottles Lucia makes for the year is about 3000. To make that sort of quantity, Lucia needs to buy the tomatoes in bulk from the Pooraka Market Merchants through her son-in-law John who runs stall 69 in the Central Market.

All summer long our household is busy — sauce making and making and crushing tomato preserve for our pizza topping for the cafe.

Lucia preserves her own olives as well, so for the months of May–July she is busy curing her olives.

It does not stop there. Lucia prefers to kill her own poultry, so throughout the year she has delivered live a few turkey, duck, pigeon and chickens so she can kill and dress them herself. The most wonderful soup and stock are made from all parts of the chicken, turkey and pigeon, including the neck and feet which give a great flavour.

Even though we do a lot of cooking at the cafe we still enjoy cooking and entertaining at home. Every Saturday, Lucia makes fresh pasta for Sunday lunch for the family, which of course is very much appreciated by us all. We usually get to share our Sunday lunches together and it often takes all afternoon so as not to rush at all. The pasta type varies from week to week — tagliatelli, spaghetti, fusilli or cavatelli. The fusilli is the most time-consuming to make and it often takes a few of us to help with the process. In fact, Lucia could spend up to three hours making the fusilli for eight people. After mixing the dough she puts it through the machine which cuts it into strips, then into one-inch rectangular pieces. Then each piece is rolled individually around a steel rod to form a closed tube — unbelievable work! This particular pasta was much loved by Lucia's husband Pasquale, who enjoyed all pasta but really appreciated the effort taken to make fusilli on special days. He is very much missed by Lucia who loved to spoil him with all his favourite flavours of her cooking.

Now here is a typical menu for our family's Sunday lunch:

Pasta alla Ragù

Braciola (usually with turkey breast)

Either pork ribs or veal with salad

The sugo made for our pasta alla ragù is flavoured with different cuts of meat — whichever is available at the time.

We nearly always have turkey included in this way: the turkey breast is used for the braciola, which is rolled up with eggs, cheese, parsley and garlic then tied with string. The turkey roll and other pieces of meat are then lightly braised in oil just to brown and seal them and then put aside.

To make the sugo at this stage, choose a saucepan big enough for the sauce to cover all of the meat. In the saucepan add the oil from the frying pan you have just fried the meat in, use 1 clove of garlic per bottle of sauce and brown. Once the garlic is golden add the tomato sauce. As tomatoes are available at this time of year we usually use a few fresh tomatoes as well as the sauce. Once the sauce comes to the boil add salt and a dash of water, then add the pieces of braised meat and the turkey roll and cook altogether for at least 2 hours. You will know when it is all cooked because the meat will be easily pierced by a fork. It is advisable to rest the sugo for a while before serving if possible but it's not necessary.

Of course, when cooking the pasta select a saucepan which will allow the pasta to be cooked in plenty of water.

While the pasta is cooking, Emma usually removes the meat out of the sugo and puts it aside to have with salad later. Lee usually grates the cheese ready for the pasta. Once the pasta is cooked and drained well, Lucia returns it to the dry saucepan where you add a little sugo and grated cheese and mix well so that all the pasta is coated with sugo. Then distribute into individual dishes and top with more sugo, grated cheese and freshly ground pepper.

Essential with pasta, of course, is red wine, of which there is always a continual supply.

Next course, after a large bowl of pasta, is never served in a hurry. The braciola is untied and then cut — it looks fantastic — great colours — the yellow and green inside the turkey roll, a piece of either pork or veal and, of course, green salad dressed with olive oil, salt and homemade vinegar.

Something that is also essential in our home is coffee! Our own blend, of course, which we also sell at Lucia's. We still have an 'Atomic' home espresso maker which we have had for at least twenty years; it makes wonderful coffee and enough steam for frothing milk for Emma's hot chocolate.

Lucia, Pasquale, Nicci and Maria were born in Pago Veiano, Benevento in Italy. What I am coming to is that our household is never without the saffron-coloured liquore called Strega (Italian for witch) which is made in Benevento. It is wonderful with coffee. It is also good in cooking to flavour cakes and biscuits.

That is our Sunday lunch, we all love it!

For the rest of the week Lucia likes to cook a variety of dishes depending on what is in season and in her garden. Mainly she uses all kinds of vegetables with occasional meat or fish, but predominantly vegetables. Lucia loves beans of all kinds — borlotti, cannellini, broad beans and green stick beans.

In summer Lucia cooks zucchini with tomato and onion or zucchini salad with oil, garlic, mint and origano; she also fries the zucchini flower coated in batter.

As well as pasta Lucia uses rice and polenta with her vegetables.

index